MODERN EL

ALAN MONTEFIORI
HIDÉ ISHIGURO, ᴄᴏLUMBIA UNIVERSITY
RAYMOND GEUSS, PRINCETON UNIVERSITY

# HUSSERL AND REALISM IN
# LOGIC AND MATHEMATICS

# HUSSERL
# AND REALISM IN LOGIC AND
# MATHEMATICS

## ROBERT S. TRAGESSER

*University of California, Riverside*

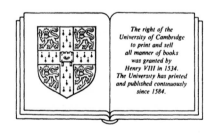

The right of the
University of Cambridge
to print and sell
all manner of books
was granted by
Henry VIII in 1534.
The University has printed
and published continuously
since 1584.

CAMBRIDGE UNIVERSITY PRESS
CAMBRIDGE
LONDON   NEW YORK   NEW ROCHELLE
MELBOURNE   SYDNEY

CAMBRIDGE UNIVERSITY PRESS
Cambridge, New York, Melbourne, Madrid, Cape Town,
Singapore, São Paulo, Delhi, Dubai, Tokyo, Mexico City

Cambridge University Press
The Edinburgh Building, Cambridge CB2 8RU, UK

Published in the United States of America by Cambridge University Press, New York

www.cambridge.org
Information on this title: www.cambridge.org/9780521285872

First published 1984
Re-issued 2011

A catalogue record for this publication is available from the British Library

Library of Congress Catalogue Card Number: 83-7631

ISBN 978-0-521-24297-4 Hardback
ISBN 978-0-521-28587-2 Paperback

FOR MY PARENTS

What if the relativity of Truth and of the evidence of Truth, on the one hand, and, on the other, the infinitely distant, ideal, absolute Truth beyond all relativity – *what if each of these has a legitimacy and each demands the other?*

(Edmund Husserl, *Formal and transcendental logic*)

I remain convinced . . . that the issue between Realism and Anti-Realism . . . is one of the most fundamental of all problems in philosophy.

(Michael Dummett, *Truth and other enigmas*)

# CONTENTS

# EDITORS' INTRODUCTION

The purpose of this series is to help to make contemporary European philosophy intelligible to a wider audience in the English-speaking world, and to suggest its interest and importance, in particular to those trained in analytical philosophy. The first book in the series was, appropriately enough, Charles Taylor's book on *Hegel and modern society*. It is by reference to Hegel that one may indicate most starkly the difference between the two traditions to whose intercommunication the series seeks to contribute; for the analytical philosophy of the contemporary Anglo-Saxon world was largely developed by Moore, Russell and others in revolt against idealism and the influence of British Hegelians at the turn of this century. It is true that the British and American idealists had themselves already diverged considerably from Hegel, but their holistic philosophy was certainly Hegelian both in terminology and in aspiration. Moore and Russell for their part obviously owed most to a different tradition stemming from Hume. Nevertheless, it should not be forgotten that they too were influenced by European contemporaries to whose writings, indeed, they explicitly appealed in their revolt against the British Hegelians. In particular they admired two European philosophers who had very little sympathy for Hegelianism: Brentano in the case of Moore, and in the case of Russell, Frege.

The next book in our series, Raymond Geuss's book on Habermas' critique of ideology, *The idea of a critical theory*, discussed issues which could be understood only by reference back to the thoughts of Hegel and Marx, which – in marked contrast to what happened in the English-speaking world – was absorbed and further developed in their own characteristic ways by the main trends of radical thought on the European continent. In England, on the other hand, philosophical opposition to 'Establishment' ways of thinking and patterns of influence was developed in opposition to Hegel rather than under his influence. In the mid-thirties, just when Hegel's philosophy was being introduced seriously to the academic world in Paris, A. J. Ayer returned from Vienna to Oxford as a champion of the logical positivism of the Vienna Circle, whose chief target of attack was precisely Hegel. It is true that logical positivism was short-lived in England; and even in the United States, to which several members of the Vienna Circle eventually escaped, it represented an important phase rather than a lasting school. But many of the philosophical virtues with which it was most concerned continued to be fostered. What is now called analytical philosophy, with its demand for thoroughness of conceptual analysis and its suspicion of rhetoric and grandiose structures, came to be more and more dominant in the English-speaking world. The philosophical attitude which it represents and which distinguishes it from the dominant European schools of thought is succinctly expressed in the foreword of the *Philosophical remarks* (1930) of Wittgenstein, whose influence on analytical philosophy was incalculable:

This spirit is different from the one which informs the vast stream of European and American civilization in which all of us stand. The spirit expresses itself in an onwards movement, in building ever larger and more complicated structures: the other in striving after clarity and perspicacity in no matter what structure . . . And so the first adds one construction to another, moving on and up, as it were, from one stage to the next, while the other remains where it is and what it tries to grasp is always the same.

Husserl and his followers in phenomenology also insisted on the need for exact description and rigor. This book by Robert Tragesser on Husserl and mathematical realism throws light on a facet of recent philosophy in Europe which has eluded the main stream of analytical philosophy while at the same time concerning itself with problems that have been central to it. Analytical philosophy of logic and language and of the foundations of mathematics was much more influenced by the thoughts of Frege who had criticized Husserl's first book on philosophy of mathematics for its psychologism. Husserl accepted much of Frege's criticism, but there were some aspects of Husserl's philosophy of mathematics which Frege did not touch and which Husserl was to develop throughout his life: the objects of our thoughts and how we think about them in general, and the objective and *a priori* grounds for the way we think about mathematical objects in particular. We are told how Husserl's view was taken seriously both by Gödel – who is often thought to be a mathematical Platonist – and by the intuitionists. Indeed what Robert Tragesser says about Husserl's view of noema (that which is thought about as we think it) and object may be seen as directly relevant to problems that still trouble us in the philosophy of mathematics, problems concerning the connection of assertability conditions and truth conditions, objectivity and realism.

Of course everyone knows that the labels 'analytical' and 'European' (or 'continental') are very unsatisfactory. There are philosophers of the phenomenological tradition working in the U.S.A., though very little in the field of philosophy of mathematics. There are many other philosophers engaged in work of conceptual analysis in the Scandinavian countries, Poland, and, more recently, Germany. Moreover, the universities of Europe which have not been influenced by the analytical tradition – and these include nearly all of those in France and Italy, and the great majority of those in German-speaking countries and in Eastern Europe – have by no means represented any unitary tradition themselves. The disagreements, or even lack of communication, between, for instance, Hegelians, Marxists, phenomenologists and Thomists have often been deep. But these disagreements are 'small' in comparison with the barriers of mutual ignorance and distrust between the main representatives of the analytical tradition on the one hand and the main philosophical schools of the European continent on the other (schools which are also dominant in Latin America, Japan and even some universities in the U.S.A. and Canada). These barriers are inevitably reinforced by the fact that, until very recently at any rate, even the best students from the universities situated on either side have tended to emerge from their studies with such divergent areas of knowledge and ignorance, competence and incompetence, that they are hardly equipped even to enter into informed discussion with one another about the nature of what separates them.

We tend, nevertheless, to forget that the erection of these barriers is a relatively recent phenomenon. Brentano, writing on the philosophy of mind at the end of the last century, made frequent reference to J. S. Mill and to other contemporary British philosophers. In turn, as we have noticed, Moore refers to Brentano. Bergson discusses William James frequently in his works. For Husserl one of the most important philosophers was Hume. The thinkers discussed seriously by Russell include not only Frege and Poincaré, but also Meinong. How unfortunate, then, that those who have followed in their footsteps have refused to read or to respect one another, the one convinced that the other survives on undisciplined rhetoric and an irresponsible lack of rigor, the other suspecting the former of aridity, superficiality and over-subtle trivialization.

The books of this series represent contributions by philosophers who have worked in the analytical tradition, but who now tackle problems specifically raised by philosophers of the main traditions to be found within contemporary Europe. They are works of philosophical argumentation and of substance rather than merely introductory résumés. We believe that they may contribute toward the formation of a richer and less parochial framework of thinking, a wider frame within which mutual criticism and stimulation will be attempted and where mutual disagreements will at least not be based on ignorance, contempt or distortion.

# PREFACE

Is the world already made or of our making? This, in metaphorical terms,[1] is the modern problem, first formulated with clarity and precision by Michael Dummett, of realism or anti-realism. In particular, Michael Dummett has seen that this is essentially a problem about the nature of thought, or rather of thoughts. He saw that the answer depends on the validity of the 'law of the excluded middle' for thoughts, the principle that thoughts are either true or false, and are true or false antecedently to our knowing which. But for Dummett, as for most philosophers within the analytic tradition, the study of thinking and of thought is exactly the study of language and its use. Yet, whether or not this principle of analytic philosophy is correct is itself something that must be established, and established with complete rigor. In order to do this, a study of the *cogito*, the 'I think' in all of its forms, is necessary.

Since Frege, philosophy has undergone a linguistic turn, and concomitantly the strategies of metaphysical inquiry have been reshaped. For Kant objects are a posit of experience, and ontology must be based on an investigation of the *a priori* conditions of experience, but after Frege being an object is understood *as a posit of the use of language*, requiring that ontology be based on an inquiry into the nature of linguistic meaning and its connections with truth. As was already evident in the writings of Bernard Bolzano, in particular his *Paradoxes of the infinite*,[2] this turn to language and the under-

---

1 This particular metaphor is due to Hilary Putnam.

2 Bernard Bolzano, *Paradoxes of the infinite*, trans. Fr Prihousky (New Haven, Conn., 1950).

lying propositions promised to liberate ontology from Kantian constraints, providing access to regions of being inaccessible to sensory experience, regions such as those populated by complete infinite totalities and infinite totalities of such totalities.

Yet the promised liberation was never fully effected: new paradoxes and antinomies arose, such as Russell's Paradox. Some tried to save the situation by various constraints or *ad hoc* devices, none fully satisfactory from a philosophical point of view, while others such as the mathematical intuitionist L. E. J. Brouwer renounced the linguistic turn, liberalizing Kantian schemata but insisting that there could be no rational positing of objects without an immanent experience exhaustively presenting them, and forcing an 'idealist' or anti-realist conception of being.

Modern 'linguistic' realism stems from Frege who argued in his *Foundations of arithmetic*[3] that arithmetic does not have a foundation in experiential intuition, thereby forcing a general account of meaning and truth which is independent of such intuition. Such an account is also and rather more straightforwardly required if, for example, one is to have *as objects* the transfinite entities contemplated by Georg Cantor. The problem of preserving both the linguistic turn and the possibility of holding with Brouwer that such a realism is essentially incoherent has been tackled by Michael Dummett. He presented the problem realism vs. anti-realism as one to be solved by an adequate theory of meaning for linguistic expression, and furthermore has made it credible that an anti-realist theory of meaning and thus truth is coherent and even correct. Dummett argues that the correct theory of meaning will impose an interpretation on linguistic expressions, providing them with a uniform interpreted logical syntax which allows and determines one, and only one, conception of truth to be associated with the sentences: one conception of truth and, correlatively, one conception of being (e.g. that of realism or anti-realism).

3 Gottlob Frege, *Foundations of arithmetic*, trans. J. L. Austin (New York, 1950).

However, the very writings which give impetus to the linguistic turn, those of Frege, suggest doubts and worries here. First, as he insisted (in e.g. 'Thoughts'),[4] Frege focused on thoughts primarily and language secondarily. Second, in his posthumously published writings Frege said that the inconsistency of his *Grundgesetze* (discovered by Russell) was a result of *thinking* being misled by *speaking* (see Frege's 'Sources of knowledge of mathematics and the mathematical natural sciences').[5] This suggests something more fundamental than language, viz. the thoughts which lie 'behind' language. Of course, it is a not altogether thoughtless skepticism about there being such objects of inquiry which encourages the linguistic turn; nonetheless there are many considerations suggesting that we should make an effort to overcome this skepticism and attempt to think about thought. There are certainly reasons to do so independently of Frege's worries about thinking being misled by speaking, although that is surely enough. Clearly thinking can outrun speaking. For example, our thoughts frame the natural numbers which have not yet been brought to adequate expression. For any system of expression, e.g. a formal system, can be rightfully construed as being satisfied by entities we recognize are not natural numbers. However, *this* recognition, or thought, does not have adequate logical expression, as we cannot pick out *the* natural numbers.

Furthermore, though on some views, such as Michael Dummett's, it is maintained that our more or less ordinary way of speaking 'contains' a conception of being or truth (e.g. that of anti-realism), nevertheless thinking *seems* to be capable of forming highly novel languages, indeed unspoken and virtually unspeakable languages which yet appear to be expressive of thoughts. We might then wonder whether thinking might not be able to mold and shape language to its needs, and perhaps even to construct languages which express or contain

4 Gottlob Frege, 'Thoughts', in his *Logical investigations*, trans. P. T. Geach and R. H. Stoothoff (Oxford, 1977).

5 Gottlob Frege, 'Sources of knowledge of mathematics and the mathematical natural sciences', in his *Posthumous writings*, trans. P. Long and R. White (Oxford, 1979).

different conceptions of being and truth, tailored to different ontological regions.

The present work explores this possibility for mathematical objects with particular emphasis on the problem of the justifiability of a realist conception of being for them. It does so through the discipline of Husserl's phenomenology, for that is a powerful theory of the *cogito*. Husserl claimed that all intentional acts of consciousness, even ordinary perceptions, have the characteristic of being directed toward objects (and are *all* instances of the *cogito*). Each has its 'noematic content', the component of thought determined by what is thought in that act, as it is thought. And Husserl's method returned to the starting point, the *cogito*, attempting to found all philosophy, including logic and ontology, on the study of noematic contents. For it is through these intelligible contents of thinking that ontological domains become manifest and known. The following chapters therefore serve as an exercise in attending to *thought* and in showing how metaphysics – or more strictly, ontology – is founded on this attention.

Husserl emphasized often that it is in the nature of the case that everyone must think phenomenology through for themselves: the field of thoughts, the noematic, is there for us all to study and investigate. There are no dogmas. Accordingly, in subsequent chapters I have taken what I consider to be the most important ideas in Husserl and have attempted to think them through afresh, employing some phenomenological analysis, but resisting taking anything wholesale from Husserl. Indeed this has been necessary, for Husserl's own writings are not perfectly adapted to a study of the problems at hand. I examine aspects of the problem of understanding and justifying a mathematical realism and develop a phenomenological critique of the law of the excluded middle and its implication that there are objective truth values. Whether or not realism with respect to mathematical domains and indeed, with respect to the world we find ourselves in, is justified will be left unsettled, but this work will have succeeded if it has in some measure clarified the status of the law of the excluded middle and has shown the way to what must be done finally in order to justify the realist attitude.

This work continues my *Phenomenology and logic* (Ithaca, N.Y., 1977), although independent of it and more systematically Husserlian.

I am deeply grateful for support from an American Council of Learned Societies Fellowship, and for valuable comments and suggestions from many people including the following: Roberta De Monticelli; series editors Hidé Ishiguro and Alan Montefiore; and the staff of Cambridge University Press.

*Wolfson College, Oxford*
1981

# ABBREVIATIONS
## (WRITINGS BY EDMUND HUSSERL)

*LI*   *Logical investigations*, trans. J. Findlay (New York, 1970): *Logische Untersuchungen* (Tübingen, 1968).

*ID*   *Ideas*, trans. W. R. B. Gibson (New York, 1969): *Ideen zu einer reinen Phänomenologie und phänomenologischen Philosophie I, Husserliana* (The Hague, 1950).

*FTL*   *Formal and transcendental logic*, trans. D. Cairns (The Hague, 1969): *Formale und transzendentale Logik, Husserliana* (The Hague, 1974).

# INTRODUCTION

## THE IDEA OF HUSSERL'S PHENOMENOLOGICAL FOUNDATION FOR LOGIC

Human reason has the peculiar fate that in one species of its knowledge it is burdened by questions which, as prescribed by the very nature of reason itself, it is not able to ignore, but which, as transcending all its powers, it is also not able to answer.

The perplexity into which it thus falls is not due to any fault of its own. It begins with principles which it has no option save to employ in the course of experience, and which this experience at the same time abundantly justifies it in using. Rising with their aid . . . to ever higher and more remote conditions, it soon becomes aware that in this way – the questions never ceasing – its work must always remain incomplete; and it therefore finds itself compelled to resort to principles which overstep all empirical employment, and yet which seem so unobjectionable that even ordinary consciousness readily accepts them. But by this procedure human reason precipitates itself into darkness and contradictions.

(Kant, *Critique of pure reason*, Preface to the first edition)

But how is *Evidenz* related to truth?
Actually the relation is not so simple.

(Husserl, *FTL*, para. 91)

In the early nineteenth century, the logician, mathematician, and theologian Bernard Bolzano turned to thought and the study of its intrinsic nature with a view to freeing thinking and reason from Kantian constraints. He sought to push back the limits beyond which 'human reason precipitates itself into darkness and contradiction'. His successes were great enough to open the way for Georg Cantor to develop his rich and powerful mathematics of the transfinite, enabling us to enter what David Hilbert regarded as a paradise from which we will not be expelled.

There was, however, a clear metaphysical assumption at the root of Bolzano's logic, an assumption which can also be found in the logic of the later Gottlob Frege, albeit in a more refined form, Frege's logical reflections being in general much more refined, while also much more limited, than those of Bolzano. The assumption on which the logic of Bolzano and Frege depended was the so-called law of the excluded middle or, alternatively, the realist conception of truth. In those of his writings with the greatest significance for the foundations of logic,[1] Edmund Husserl may be construed as attempting to purge logical thinking of this assumption while at the same time avoiding the pitfalls of psychologism. He endeavored to sustain the claim of reason to advance beyond the limits Kant fixed for it in confining it to the field of empirical and pure intuition, without any such 'dangerous' metaphysical assumptions.

The assumption can be described quite simply. Bolzano in his *Theory of science*[2] maintained that there are propositions-in-themselves which are either true or false. They are in no way dependent on us for their being, and they are true or false independently of, and antecedently to, our judging them to be so. He also expressed this fact by claiming that these propositions exist in the mind of God. Bolzano also maintains a correspondence theory of truth. For Bolzano, to every true proposition, there corresponds a state of affairs in the world, and to every state of affairs in the world, there corresponds a true proposition.

In his late essay 'Thoughts', Frege maintains that there is a 'third realm' whose members are *thoughts*, analogues of Bolzano's propositions-in-themselves. Thoughts are grasped and judged by us, but have a life of their own independent of us. In particular, they are true or false, and, more importantly, true or false antecedently to our either grasping or judging them.

In contrast to Bolzano, Frege does not maintain a correspondence theory of truth. He argues that what it means for a thought to be true cannot be explained in terms of a corre-

1 Namely, *LI, ID* and *FTL*.

2 Bernard Bolzano, *Theory of science*, ed. Jan Berg, trans. Burnham Terrell (Boston, Mass., 1973).

spondence with the world, for such an explanation will inevitably require a utilization of the notion of truth. More deeply, he points out that understanding that the thought expressed by 'Milan is north of Pisa' is true amounts to no more than understanding that Milan is north of Pisa. That is, 'Milan is north of Pisa' is true if, and only if, Milan is north of Pisa. We cannot say more than this (the redundancy theory of truth).

The difference between Bolzano and Frege amounts to a disavowal by Frege of the presumption of 'the absolute point of view'. *We* cannot grasp the structure of the world except by grasping true thoughts; whereas for a correspondence theory of truth an independent grasp of the structure of the world is essential. We cannot grasp the world either antecedently to or independently of thoughts in the third realm.

There are three difficulties with the conception of the third realm. First, there is a problem of deciding when we have grasped a thought in this realm, of deciding when we have constructed a sentence expressive of a thought which is true or false independently of us. Second, there is a problem about the sense in which such thoughts have being. Third, there is the problem of how we can be certain that they determine objective reality, reality not dependent on our thinking and experience. There is a residual Platonism here, or a residuum of the absolute point of view.

More or less addressing these problems, Hermann Lotze wrote:

Only a mind which stood at the center of the real world, not outside individual things but penetrating them with its presence, could command such a view of reality that left nothing to look for . . . But the human mind, with which we are concerned, does not stand at the center of things, but has a modest position somewhere in the extreme ramifications of reality . . . However much . . . we may presuppose an original reference of the forms of thought to the nature of things which is the goal of knowledge, we must be prepared to find in them many elements which do not directly reproduce the actual reality to the knowledge of which they are to lead us.[3]

3 Hermann Lotze, *Logic*, trans. B. Bosanquet (Oxford, 1898), para. IX.

Indeed, throughout the remainder of his *Logic* and in his metaphysical writings, Lotze can be read as adducing more and more reasons which could be used to establish the conviction that a realm of thoughts of the sort Frege posited has no being for us.

The writings of Lotze, although of course available before Frege, remind us of a difficulty for those who would like to defend Frege's view by maintaining that *we* form thoughts, perhaps doing so by an increasingly refined development and use of our language. If thoughts are of our making, we have no guarantee that they are true or false antecedently to our judging them to be either true or false, no guarantee that they have anything to do with objective truth (truth not dependent on our thinking and experience). If we can only be sure that they are true or false after we have either judged them to be true or judged them to be false, then we have no guarantee that 'truth' means more than, say, 'acceptable' or 'validated', that 'truth' has anything at all to do with objective reality, or with any realm of being not of our making, and independent of us. To make the point clearer, consider for a moment a set of sentences *S*. Choose some arbitrary but consistent set of those sentences and regard a sentence as 'acceptable' or 'validated' if it can be deduced from these last sentences. There is no reason whatsoever to expect that the acceptable set of sentences have anything to do with objective reality. If thoughts are of our making, there is no reason to believe that the thoughts we find ourselves willing to accept have any more to do with objective reality than those sentences accepted in our example. It might just be that the principles of acceptance or validation are quite obscure, but at root just as arbitrary. If we cannot be certain that the thoughts we accept are either true or false antecedently to our finding them acceptable, we are that far from being certain that they have anything to do with objective reality.

Although more or less neutral on the matter in his *LI*, by the time of his *FTL* Husserl is quite explicitly saying that senses (*Sinne*), such as sentential senses, are of our making. It is the very essence of thinking to constitute senses. In that work he confronts the problem of the possibility and sense of objective truth, given that we constitute senses. It is my purpose in this work to develop the basis for a phenomenological solution to this problem.

A minimal condition that sentential senses are true of objective reality is that they are true antecedently to our knowing that they are. The problem we confront is that of knowing that the sentential senses associated with some language are true or false antecedently to our knowing for each whether it is true or whether it is false. This is the main concern of Chapters 1 and 5. A solution to the problem requires an analysis of the nature of senses, and indeed Husserl's phenomenology *narrowly* viewed has as its end the achievement within a much wider enterprise, the development of the theory of the '*cogito*', the 'I think', in all its forms and manifestations. Phenomenology begins as a descriptive theory of the noematic, a descriptive theory of what is thought in acts of thought as it is thought. While this is where phenomenology begins, its aim is to develop a theoretical characterization of the domain of all possible thoughts and thus also all possible entities which can be thought. Only by beginning descriptively and proceeding by careful generalizations can one avoid introducing unwarranted metaphysical assumption, such as Frege's concerning the existence of the third realm composed of thoughts with objective truth values.

Husserl began his serious work in life as a student of mathematics under the influence of Karl Weierstrass. Weierstrass had seen (as had Bolzano) that geometric intuition did not provide an adequate basis for mathematical analysis, seeking arithmetic as a basis instead. The realization of this program of the arithmetization of analysis, if it was to be truly rigorous, desperately required a philosophical clarification of the fundamental concepts of mathematics, such as number. In particular, it required a logical clarification that shows the proper principles of reasoning, and not a metaphysical clarification. The genuine needs of the sciences, not the satisfaction of human wonder in some ethereal mystical respect, guided Husserl in his gradually developing philosophical interests. In no small part because of this, Husserl was attracted to the theories of Franz Brentano, the philosopher and psychologist who was attempting to found philosophy, and thus logic, epistemology, and value theory on psychology.

Under the influence of Brentano's way of doing philosophy, Husserl set out to construct a foundation for arithmetic, planning to clarify the concept of number by tracing its psychological origin. The result was his *Philosophie der Arithmetik* (he planned a second volume on the philosophy of geometry). In this work he criticized Frege's *Foundations of arithmetic* in a way which showed that he had failed to appreciate it. But under the influence of a sharp review of Husserl's work by Frege, followed by Husserl's recognition that his method of clarifying the concept of number could not adequately ground the principles of arithmetic – its logic[4] – Husserl saw that the major task before him was nothing less than a philosophical clarification of logic, and this by a more or less intrinsic analysis of thought, not a psychological or otherwise reductive analysis.

Although Husserl read Frege's writings and entered into correspondence with him, he looked to Bolzano's *Theory of science* (introduced to him by Georg Cantor when they were together at Halle) for a sweeping vision of the nature of logic. There Bolzano treated logic as a branch of epistemology. (It was this work that inspired Husserl's characterization of philosophy as the science of science, a science not reducible to any other, such as psychology.)

While, as Bolzano scholar Jan Berg observed, Bolzano presented 'a profoundly intensional, non-linguistic approach to logic' with a sufficiently refined articulation for it to be readily reconstructed by means of Tarskian semantical techniques,[5]

---

4 cf. Dallas Willard, 'Husserl on a logic that failed', *Philosophical Review*, vol. 89, no. 1 (1980), pp. 46–64.

5 See Jan Berg, *Bolzano's logic* (Stockholm, n.d. but *circa* 1968), especially Chapter II; for an overview see Bernard Bolzano, *Theory of science*, especially 'The editor's introduction'.

Husserl faced a serious barrier. He confronted the problem of
how to interpret without metaphysics Bolzano's metaphysical
conceptions, such as 'proposition-in-itself and 'truth-in-
itself'.

The idea for an interpretation of Bolzano's logic which
would free it from such conceptions was provided by the non-
metaphysical interpretation of Platonic ideas and judgements
or thoughts given in Lotze's *Logic*.[6]

By providing an honest and careful account and appraisal of
ratiocinative thinking, Lotze hoped to show that reality-in-
itself was inaccessible to such thinking. His motivation for
doing this was a way of rescuing the human individual in its
individuality, the human monad, from its complete assimilation to and loss in the Hegelian World-Historical *Geist* (and,
for that matter, in the natural sciences). In effect, as I hinted
above, Lotze argued that sentential senses did not have objective reality, but only 'validity' (*Geltung*). The word used by
Lotze which is translated 'reality' is *Wirklichkeit*. To be 'real' in
this sense is to be *wirklich*, to act and/or to be acted upon. It
might seem strange to describe their mode of being as 'validity',
but just as one uses *Wirklichkeit* to describe the mode of being
of *wirklich* entities in terms of the nature of their behavior, so
Lotze calls the mode of being of sentential senses 'validity'
because they confer 'validity' or 'acceptability' on (or withhold
it from) our thinking about what they purport to be about.
'Validity' here does not mean truth ('objective reality'); it simply
means a piece of thinking as being of a nature prescribed by
the sentential sense, just as the rules of derivation or inference
in a pure formal system validate certain formal strings as being
'theorems' in the formal system without any pretension of
conferring objective truth on the theorems. We are accus-
tomed to applying 'validity' to principles of reasoning. Lotze's
(and subsequently Husserl's) use is different: one is given
principles for accepting sentences. Sentences accepted on the
basis of those principles are spoken of as 'having validity'.

6 cf. Edmund Husserl, *Introduction to the logical investigations – a draft preface (1913)*,
trans. P. J. Bossert and C. H. Peters (The Hague, 1975).

Meaning by 'objective truth', 'being true of a world or domain of objects which are not dependent on us for their existence', we can raise the question of when principles conferring validity on a sentence assure that it is objectively true.

Suppose, for example, that we are given a language *L*, each sentence of which has its sentential sense and that these senses provide conditions of acceptance or validation. Suppose that through our thinking and experience we have made a great number of those sentences acceptable. But how do we know that those sentences describe or frame something which is objectively real, that they express objective truths? For that matter, what is the very meaning of 'objectively real'? We say vaguely 'exists independently of us'. Thus we expect that truths framing independent existence should be true independently of us. But what is it to be true independently of us? In some measure by postulating a third realm composed of thoughts having objective truth values, Frege avoided this question. But once we grant that *we* constitute thoughts, we must answer it, and it seems that the only way of answering is to look to the realm of possible thoughts that we can constitute and see if we can find some characteristic which such thoughts might have which would assure that if they are true, they are true independently of us, and so meet the minimum conditions for framing an objective reality. We shall discuss these matters in Chapter 1. We shall see that it is not enough to ensure that a sentence such as 'Milan is north of Pisa' is objectively true or false that it appears to be obvious that 'Milan is north of Pisa' is true if, and only if, Milan is north of Pisa, for the 'obviousness' may be an illusion engendered by not attending with sufficient care to the full sentential sense (for example it might be the case that if we attended to that sense carefully enough we would see that the right-hand side requires an expression of verification conditions).

In order to discover properties which principles of validation should have in order to assure that sentences on which they confer validity are objectively true, we must undertake a study of the domain of all possible sense-formations or, at least, of their source, the *cogito*.

This discussion prepares us for the three fundamental steps which put Husserl on the road to pure phenomenology (or transcendental phenomenology):
(1) The radical readjustment of Brentano's act psychology. During this period psychology was receiving enormous impetus from the work of Wilhelm Wundt and Hermann Helmholtz. They were developing a physiological psychology. Behind their work was the premiss that the life of the mind could ultimately be understood on such a foundation, that is, on the foundations of experimentally studied and founded laws of sensation and association, even higher functions such as thinking. Against this movement and its historical precedents Brentano instituted act psychology, a study of the intrinsic structure of mental acts which seeks an understanding of them which does not proceed by reducing them to physiological structures. Included in the domain are all acts of thinking, judgement, perception, observation, volition, valuation, and so on. At first tacitly and later with an explicit methodology called 'the phenomenological reduction', Husserl established a way of framing and studying the domain of acts of consciousness. Roughly, one was to proceed 'phenomenologically', to bring to increasingly perfect description acts and their contents just as they presented themselves to introspection without the use of auxiliary hypotheses drawn either from the sciences or from metaphysics. In particular, Husserl tried to frame the method of description in just such a way that one considered and brought out exactly and only those features of the acts useful to and significant for thinking.

Husserl's methodological reductions were aimed at isolating and bringing out just those features of mental acts which were relevant to further thinking about the purported objects toward which such acts are directed. Husserl was convinced that those features were essentially transparent to introspection, and accessible only to introspection and that otherwise they would be of no use to thinking.

By such introspection one finds that there are predicate senses, sentential senses, and so on. Indeed, as Husserl notes in his *LI*,[7] they *seem* to have a life of their own independent of what Husserl called the *reell* aspects of acts of consciousness, e.g. features binding them to the moment in which they are thought, their being thought through a particular sentence, and so on. But this seeming independence is not a metaphysical independence, but a misinterpretation of the repeatability of sense-constituting thinking. In thinking we constitute senses. We can repeatedly constitute the same sense. But we may misinterpret this repeated constituting as a repeated encountering of a sense which is always already there, by this misinterpretation preparing the ground for believing in something like Frege's third realm. There is no ground here for the belief that such senses frame '*the* objectively real world'; indeed, it is virtually a consequence of the thesis that we constitute or construct senses that there is no such privileged collection of senses, although Husserl did not draw this conclusion.

Particular acts of consciousness bound to one person and one time can never occur again, but their 'contents', e.g. their element of sense, their propositional content, can be so-to-speak utilized repeatedly by different acts over widely separated times, acts performed even by different persons. Such contents, thoughts, are present to mind and they can be unfolded in various ways, their structure studied, and so on. If they could not, then they would indeed be useless to thinking. Husserl believed that as far as their relevance to thinking is concerned, no metaphysics or psychology should be invoked to study and understand them. The reason is that their use to thinking is completely exhausted by what their analysis provides.

(2) Husserl believed that the intensional contents of acts of consciousness had a close connection with the concept of

7 cf. especially *LI*, Investigation I.

validity. That is, it is in their nature to prescribe the conditions of their 'validation'. Precisely because metaphysical considerations are not allowed and because one cannot ascribe to thoughts more than one has found in them (e.g. conditions of validation) Husserl could not regard the law of the excluded middle as obviously true since this principle requires the ascription of objective truth values to thoughts. In part because of this, Husserl could not follow Frege in his formal development of classical quantificational logic as *the* logic of truth.

(3) Inspired in some measure by Bolzano, Husserl confronted the problem of Lotze's claims of the inaccessibility of the real-in-itself to thought in the following way: he regarded such a conception as simply vacuous. He thought it absurd to claim to be able to think in any way about something whose nature is such that we cannot think about it. But, more importantly, there is a sense we can give to 'the real-in-itself' or 'the real world' that enables us to pursue it as an object of thought, viz. what the sciences try to disclose. Husserl recalls that it is an ideal of the sciences to disclose that which we reach through thought by constantly striving to divest thinking of the subjective, of having as objects of thought entities dependent on our mental performances for their being. The first task of logic *qua* the science of the sciences is to investigate the nature of mental performances, mental acts, acts of consciousness, seeking to determine how and in what sense we can have as objects of consciousness and thought entities not dependent for their being on our consciousness and thinking. For us, in the present work, this investigation will take the form of determining when the satisfaction of conditions of validation or acceptance guarantees objective truth. Let us now look at the notion of conditions of validation more closely.

For Husserl, acts of consciousness are intentional;[8] they have the character of being directed toward, of being concerned

8 What he actually says is that acts of consciousness 'in the pregnant sense' are intentional. This is just a way of indicating that, whatever other sorts of acts of consciousness there might be, it is only the intentional acts which are of interest to him.

with, objects. Each such act contains an element of thought, viz. that by which the purported object of the act is thought. The element of thought in such an act Husserl refers to as *the noema* of the act. To describe it is to describe the object of thought as it is thought in that act, e.g. how it is framed, what is ascribed to it in what manner. We cannot grasp, apprehend, or otherwise be conscious of an object other than on the basis of noemata framing the purported objects of consciousness, just as for Frege, in his rejection of the correspondence theory of truth, we cannot grasp the world save through sentential senses.

Now with every noema there are associated relations of 'fulfillability'. These relations are relations between acts of consciousness and various kinds of senses which may be ingredients in the noema. When the sense is analogous to the sense of a singular term such as 'the river Cherwell', the relation of fulfillability works to determine which acts of perception, observation, and even imagination can count as presentations of, or, in the last case, a pictorial image of, the thing or sort of thing indicated. The relation of fulfillability may be capable of being so tightened that it determines which acts present exactly what is indicated. There are analogous relations of fulfillability for predicate and relational senses.

Likewise also for sentential senses: the associated relations of fulfillability condition an analogously full range of acts of consciousness, varying from acts of imagination giving what it would be like to see that the river Cherwell is a winding river to acts of consciousness (perhaps very complex) justifying our asserting that the river Cherwell is a winding river. 'Fulfillability' even extends to acts of consciousness (reflection) presenting chains of inferences to the conclusion that such and such is the case. That is, among conditions of 'fulfillability' are conditions of what I have been calling 'validation' ('validation' or 'acceptance' displaces 'fulfilment' in Husserl's *FTL*).

Very roughly speaking, the complex of fulfillability relations implicated in a noema determines what acts of consciousness have some bearing on being determinative of the thought object as thought (the meant object as meant, the intended object as intended), determining exactly what bearing they have on this determination (e.g. from being an imaginative illustration of it to providing grounds for justifiably asserting something about it).

Now let us suppose that one is thinking about a particular 'ontological region' (Husserl's term) such as 'the natural world', or 'the domain of natural numbers', or 'the domain of poetry', or whatever. There will be a noematic core common to all such acts of thought which will provide a fulfillability relation. In particular this core provides what I have been characterizing as relations of 'validity'. For an ontological region $O$, let us refer to such a relation as '$Val_O$'. We write '$Val_O(A, S)$', where $A$ is a mental act of mental performance and $S$ is a sentence. To assert that $Val_O(A, S)$ is to assert that an occurrence of $A$ validates $S$, confers acceptability on $S$. The validation of $S$ *depends* on the occurrence of $A$. Our fundamental problem is to determine conditions a $Val_O$ must satisfy in order for us to be justified in regarding the validated sentences as being objectively true, as being true independently of our validations, of our mental performances, as having objective truth values.

In a liberal sense, a $Val_O$ provides *the principles for reasoning* about the ontological region $O$, i.e. the principles telling us which mental performances and which acts of consciousness used in what ways lead to 'validated' assertions. A $Val_O$ is entirely a function of what we mean by $O$, as a function of the noemata on whose basis we think about $O$. If this meaning is defective, if we cannot genuinely mean something by it, then $Val_O$ will be defective. Perhaps $Val_O$ allows for us to be justified in accepting $S$ and also not-$S$. Or perhaps an analysis of $Val_O$ will reveal that there are admitted questions $S?$ for which it is impossible *to conceive* of an act $A$ such that either $Val_O(A, S)$ or $Val_O(A, not-S)$. In such cases the purported domain falls short of what Husserl called 'true being', viz.:

To every object 'that truly is' there intrinsically corresponds . . . the idea of a possible consciousness (perhaps infinitary) in which the object itself can be grasped in a perfectly adequate way. Conversely, when this possibility is guaranteed, the object is *eo ipso* 'that which truly is'. (*ID*, para. 142)

The 'perfectly adequate way' is just the achieved mental acts or mental performances $A$ such that, for relevant sentences $S$, $\text{Val}_O(A, S)$.

Although I have referred to an ontological region $O$ in my discussion, the idea of 'true being' applies equally well to a purported object within an ontological region.

As we shall see in subsequent chapters, when the 'true being' of $O$ is assured, then validity coincides with truth, perhaps indeed objective truth, truth in the realist sense of Bolzano and Frege.

The logic and, indeed the epistemology of an ontological region is completely founded on $\text{Val}_O$. It is thus $\text{Val}_O$ and the securing of $O$ as having 'true being' (in a sense to be spelled out more fully in subsequent chapters) which may *justify* a Fregean logic, thereby fully clarifying and validating its sense.

If I were forced to state simply and suggestively the fundamental principle or thesis underlying Husserlian phenomenology, it would be this:

*no entity (for us) antecedently to a way of thinking and to thinking in that way*

For 'a way of thinking' one might substitute 'principles of reasoning', 'principles of validation (a $\text{Val}_O$)', or even 'a discourse'. According to this thesis, we are not first given entities and afterwards confront the problem of how to think about them. Rather, whatever entities are there for us, they are made present to our minds, to our consciousness, by our thinking in accordance with an antecedently given way of thinking, in accordance with antecedently given principles of reasoning, validation. This principle gives the essence of Husserl's 'theory of intentionality', his so-called 'theory of constitution'. Our problem is to discover a way of thinking presenting the objectively real, a way of thinking whose validations coincide with objective truth. If I focus mainly on mathematics and the problem of the 'objective reality' of mathematical entities, that is because it seems inevitable that any domain of senses framing the objectively real will draw upon mathematics. If the mathematics drawn upon is not a body of 'objective truths', it is hard to see how the senses drawing upon mathematics could have sufficient integrity to frame objective truths, truths about 'an objectively real world'.

In Chapter 4 I shall principally focus on elementary topological and geometric entities. The question asked is, Can they be taken to be objectively real? Before this question can be answered, we must determine how and in what sense they are objects of thought. The Kantian solution that Euclidean geometric figures are objects of pure intuition presents some serious problems. First of all, we can only represent such figures in what is essentially empirical intuition or imagination, e.g. we draw lines in imagination. The problem here is that these drawings do not form Euclidean figures, e.g. lines have width. In particular, for such figures the principle of the transitivity of equality, the principle that two things equal to the same thing are equal to each other, fails for such figures. For example, we could have drawn triangles

$$T_1, T_2, \ldots T_n$$

such that we agree that $T_1$ is equal to $T_2$, $T_2$ is equal to $T_3$, and so on, but $T_1$ is not equal to $T_n$ because small undetectable increments of difference add up to a detectable difference between $T_1$ and $T_n$. What, then, gives us a grip on the Euclidean figures and why should the drawn figures play any role at all? As Kant observes, we use the drawn figures to guide us in our proofs, and we are not misled by those aspects of the drawn figures which deviate from the Euclidean figures, e.g. the width of the drawn lines. But how do we avoid being misled in this way? Is Kant's 'pure intuition' anything more than a faculty postulated to account for our ability to do geometry? We shall confront the problem generated by Berkeley to the effect that it is hard to see how anything intuitable by us is 'objectively real', to see how an entity as intuited has a life of its own independent of its being intuited without an appeal to the Berkeleian God. We shall find reason to believe that Euclidean figures are not objects of intuition in a Kantian sense. Husserl provides us with a way of understanding intuition of such mathematical objects that is logically independent of an assertion of their objective reality. Essentially, such intuitions are what Husserl called 'founded acts of consciousness' (*LI*, Investigation VI). To be 'founded' in this case is to be 'non-independent' of, say, visual experiences of drawings, but those visual experiences are given an altered sense, are 're-interpreted', and this, as we shall see, by instituting a new way of thinking about them, by introducing principles of reasoning different from those cogent and valid for visually experienced objects.

# 1

# ON MEANING AND THE REAL

'Husserlian phenomenology is the study and theory of the thought as thought.' Relying on the overview provided by the Introduction, it is the purpose of this chapter to begin replacing that heuristic discussion by considerations focusing us on such thoughts as objects of investigation. The approach to this field of such objects is determined by the nature of what we wish to learn from its study. The problem I shall focus on is that of determining the meaning of 'objectively real'. This chapter will be devoted to an explanation of what Husserl regarded as the essential starting point of ontological thinking, 'the bracketing of existence', which simultaneously brings into view 'the thought as thought', or the noematic, which will be explored in subsequent chapters.

Let us then begin by considering the two principal uses of 'being real'. One use is to refer to what exists primarily (irreducibly)[1] the other to refer to what does not depend on our minds for its existence.

To take the first use first, it is not hard to find in our history philosophers who said or who might have said, albeit a little less simply:

> Only water is real.
> Only numbers are real.
> Only substances are real.
> Only sensory ideas are real.
> Only physical objects are real.

---

1 cf. Michael Dummett, 'Realism', in his *Truth and other enigmas* (London, 1978).

Under these theses any entity can have more than merely apparent or illusory existence only to the extent that it can be viewed as reducible to, or as being built up from, what is taken to exist primarily. Such a theory is presented through arguments for what exists primarily or is 'real', accompanied by more or less explicit principles of reduction or construction in terms of which other entities are analyzed. It is clear that a necessary condition for such a theory is that it has available the resources to analyze every entity, resources enabling one to show that all non-real purported entities are fictional, illusory, or in some other way misbegotten by a trick of the mind. A theory which fails to show that can therefore be refuted. But nonetheless, the idea that in each such metaphysical view there lurks an important truth is compelling and, while one is not able to defend any one of them successfully, none can be completely jettisoned. In which case, how is a beginning to be made?

The idea emerges in Husserl, somewhat in the Cartesian spirit, of not making a beginning by making a choice from among metaphysical theories, but by seeking a metaphysically neutral ground from which all such theories can be evaluated. Husserl did not proceed by the method of doubt, but recommended a radically different approach.

Even brief reflection reveals an enormous variety of objects of thought: trees, stars, personalities, civilizations, poems, numbers, infinite sets, demons, gods, emotions, acts of violence and love, persons alive and dead, pi mesons. Each of these is worthy of serious attention in its own right, and any theory of the kind I have described above must account for and provide the means for evaluating all of these purported objects. In particular, it must establish the sense in which they may be said to exist: many seem to require very different means of being apprehended and thought about. It is not only their diversity which must be accounted for, but the very nature of the development of human thought, the irregular shifts of conceptual background, which themselves contribute shifts of conceptual background, which themselves contribute to the proliferation of apparent entities.

In the face of such diversity it would seem to require a special sort of madness or insensitivity to think that an adequate metaphysics of the sort described above is at all possible. Not only must we despair with Husserl (*ID*, Preface) of making an adequate choice among metaphysics, but one despairs of there being any grounds for the hope of finding a way to bring about a choice by some fresh act of understanding.

But in this very description of the problems any metaphysician confronts, we find the hint of an idea of how to make a beginning. Not, perhaps, the beginning of a metaphysics, but the beginning of a path to a standpoint from which to evaluate any metaphysics, even to the source of an understanding so deeply and completely satisfactory that the achievement of an adequate metaphysics, even were it possible, would be superfluous.

Metaphysical neutrality demands that we consider objects as only purported objects. (Any metaphysician must admit the possibility of such a standpoint, for otherwise he would be committed to taking all seeming or apparent objects as existing.) When I speak of the purported typewriter I am typing on, my way of speaking suggests that I have some doubt about the existence of the typewriter. This might be so, but to consider 'the purported typewriter' rather than the typewriter does not entail that I doubt the existence of a typewriter before me. 'Anything' of which I am conscious is surely a purported object, a purported object which may be an existing object.

The first step to phenomenology is to focus on the field of 'purported objects', setting aside questions of whether or not a considered 'purported object' is an existing object. But this is a clumsy way of speaking. I will try to do a little better.

For the sake of simplicity, a simplicity adequate to my purposes in this work, let us focus on a special category of 'purported objects', the posited objects. Whenever 'an object' comes to our attention, it is a posited object, posited by us, posited in mental acts, acts of consciousness. Positing is a necessary condition for the recognition of existing objects, for rational decisions about questions of existence will typically take the form of evaluations of positings.

This may suggest that the first step toward finding a neutral standpoint from which to evaluate any metaphysics is to undertake a study of the field of posited objects, but this is doubly incoherent. First, talk of 'the field' is problematic, for it varies with individuals and time. Second, and more importantly, such talk gives the impression that there is so to speak a world of exactly 'the posited objects'. But such a world would be so incoherent that nothing would come of introducing it into our considerations. Rather, what our attention should be drawn toward are the positings, our positing activities in acts of consciousness.

For every positing, there is '*what* is posited'. The first thesis that puts us on the path to Husserlian phenomenology is that in the case of each positing the 'what', or that which determines *what* is posited, is provided by thought, by intellection. It is what thought provides in order to think something: a concept or a meaning.

Let us, with Husserl, call this so to speak material of a positing act, the material which intellect or thought provides which makes the positing a positing of 'this object' rather than 'that object',

noema[2]

The following simple observations about positings allow us to make some preliminary inferences about the nature of noemata:

(1) Noemata somehow frame 'the objects' posited through them or on their basis.
(2) For most posited objects (such as 'this typewriter'), they are somehow framed as having more to them (e.g. more aspects or properties) than the framing makes definite. Thus it is possible that if a posited object happens to be an object, if, that is, 'it'

2 The theory of noemata is developed at length in *ID*.

exists, it could be posited on the basis of noemata framing 'the same thing' in quite different ways.

(3) For most posited or purported objects, we typically know how to ask fitting questions about them.

(4) For most such questions we know how to go about answering them in the right way. That is, we know how to go about securing 'truths' about the posited object.

Thus there is something about noemata which frames the posited object and provides a basis for thinking about, reasoning about, the posited object.

Noemata are achievements of thinking. They are, in a liberal sense, *thoughts*. In this and in later chapters I shall attempt to illuminate the structure of noemata. In order to inspire such deeper studies, let us consider now how and in what respects the study of noemata provides a foundation for the evaluation of metaphysics. In order to bring out the relevance of such a study to this problem more clearly, I will shift my point of view on the field of positings to those special episodes of what Husserl called 'intentional consciousness' (cf., e.g., *ID*, Chapter 1) or object directed consciousness.

For most mental acts in which an object is posited there is the appearance (which may or may not be an illusion) that our minds are directed toward such an object. There might not be such an object, in which case the appearance is an illusion. This phenomenon occurs for most of us even in the case of 'square circles': we seem to be able to direct our minds toward these, to think about, and even to accumulate what seem to be justified assertions about square circles, even though we know, perhaps by accumulating such contradictory justified assertions (their areas are given by both the formula for the area of a circle and by the formula for the area of a square), that square circles are impossible. It is clear from his 'The theory of objects' that this phenomenon impressed Alexius Meinong very strongly, to the point of regarding square circles as objects, albeit as objects beyond being and non-being.[3] The

---

3 Alexius Meinong, 'The theory of objects', in *Realism and the background of phenomenology*, ed. R. M. Chisholm (New York, 1960).

'seeming' here is a form of illusion not unlike optical illusions such as the Frazer spirals to be discussed in Chapter 3: even though I know that I am suffering an illusion, I cannot make the illusion go away, although I can avoid being taken in by it. Thus it is also that something as obviously impossible as a square circle nevertheless can *seem* to be an object toward which one can direct some thinking and reasoning.

It is in any case for such appearances of being that questions of existence and questions about what exists *primarily* (recall the opening of the chapter) arise. The field of such appearances, like the field of positings, and, indeed, the field of episodes of intentional consciousness generally, thus provides us with what any metaphysics which sets itself the task of deciding what exists primarily, of what 'is real' in this sense, must take into account.

If a metaphysician's decisions about what exists primarily are to be fully rational, he must begin with the field of appearances and apply to its members *some uniform criterion for the justifiability of assertions of existence*, some criterion for deciding which appearances are illusions. This criterion must have a certain independence in that one should not be able to tell without applying the criterion to the field of appearances which objects exist, e.g. one should not be able to see by looking at them that physical objects exist. Furthermore, we should not in applying it make use of anything beyond what is left after 'bracketing', anything beyond the field of appearances.

Husserl proposed such a criterion, a criterion for determining the justifiability of asserting that some posited object 'truly is'. It was discussed in the Introduction and will be further considered in Chapter 5; but here the idea is presented in its simplest terms.

As I pointed out (but it is a point to be more carefully investigated in Chapters 3 and 4), noemata on whose basis objects are posited provide criteria for determining which activities can count as correct reasoning about the purported objects and for determining which mental acts yield truths about the purported objects (should they exist).

Husserl's criterion for the justified assertability of the existence of a posited object is (to use my own words) the following:

We are justified in asserting that a posited object is an existing object to the extent that we have and are accumulating justified assertions[4] about it, to the extent that we can see that we can go on to accumulate further justified assertions, and to the extent that we can see that the accumulated justified assertions are, and will continue to be, mutually consistent and coherent.

To the extent that we can do this, to that extent we are justified in taking the posited object to be an existing object and *we are justified in taking the justified assertions to be truths*. (This is in accord with the discussion of 'truth' in the Introduction.)

As I shall explain, since this is a criterion for the *justifiability* of assertions of existence (as well as a criterion for taking 'justified assertions' as truths) rather than a criterion for existence and truth outright, it presents us with the problem of having objects as *real* (in the second sense mentioned at the beginning of this chapter), of having objects as existing independently of us and of our states of mind, for the criterion seems to be neutral in this respect. But before considering this problem I want to describe very briefly some of the problems which must be solved by any metaphysician.

Suppose that a metaphysician wants to justify the assertion that only objects of kind $K$ exist primarily (are real in our first sense). The metaphysician must first establish that there are objects of kind $K$, and this on the basis of the criterion for the justifiability of assertions of existence. Then he must argue that all other objects which might later be justifiably asserted to exist are reducible to objects of kind $K$. No reduction (such as mountains to sensory ideas) can be justified unless the reduction is perfectly faithful to the object as intended, as noematically framed or meant. It is very difficult to see how such a reduction could be achieved unless the knowledge of

4 Or, more properly, in the sense of the Introduction, 'validated or accepted sentences'.

the considered objects enables us to demonstrate that they are reducible to objects of kind $K$.

Furthermore, it is obvious from the criterion for the justifiability of assertions of existence that a necessary condition for being *fully and perfectly* justified in asserting the existence of a purported object is that one has secured full knowledge of it. In some cases, perhaps for physical objects, this could be a virtually infinite enterprise. Thus we could not obtain a fully sound and secure foundation for metaphysics independently of such knowledge.

We sketched a uniform criterion for the justifiability of assertions of existence (although it is a criterion which allows the importation of different conceptions of being, *Seinsinne*). A very natural question to ask in the face of such a criterion is, What does it mean for something to exist? *Only* that we are justified in asserting its existence? Does it mean only that our knowledge can continue to build, and continue to build with coherence and consistency? It is with these questions that the second notion of 'being real' mentioned at the beginning of this chapter acquires interest. To be real under this notion, which is properly a *Seinsinn*, a conception of being, is to exist, but to exist independently of us, of our states of mind, of our knowledge, of what we might be justified in asserting. In contrast, to be, in the anti-realist sense of the word, is to be dependent on us, on our states of mind, on knowledge, on what we are justified in asserting.

Now we have no means of ascribing or asserting existence save on the basis of that sketched criterion. Suppose that we find ourselves justified in asserting that $X$ exists. There are two questions we might want to ask about $X$, viz:

(A) *Must* $X$ be thought of as existing independently of our finding ourselves justified in asserting its existence?
(B) *Can* $X$ be thought of as existing independently of our finding ourselves justified in asserting its existence?

The necessity involved in (A) is indeed profoundly puzzling; it requires that we give a content to 'existence' which is much stronger than I can now see how to give. I shall be content in the present work to explore (B), which in any case forms necessary spadework for understanding (A).

Under what conditions can such an $X$ be coherently and consistently thought of as existing independently of our finding ourselves justified in asserting its existence? Certainly we expect that much depends on what $X$ is meant to be, on the noema on whose basis $X$ is posited. Of course it is completely unsatisfying if $X$ is simply and straightforwardly meant to be 'independently existing', as unsatisfying as adding an axiom to an axiomatic system asserting that the system is consistent. We have to find some way of understanding 'independently of us' in terms of features of noemata. But how?

Return to our sketched criterion for the justifiability of assertions of existence. We are justified in asserting the existence of $X$ to the extent that we are accumulating only justified assertions about it (and more). Notice also that we are justified in regarding those assertions as truths to the extent that we can see that they form a coherent and consistent whole and will form such a whole with future justified assertions. (As a simple example of how it could happen that justified assertions diverge from truth, consider for example the purported object, the square circle. One is justified in asserting that 'it' is a square and that 'it' is a circle, but, within the intended context of elementary geometry, one can draw a contradiction from these; the assertions, though justified, are not truths.)

The question about whether $X$ can be understood as existing independently of our being justified in asserting that it does thus reduces to the question of whether the questions we might raise or which could in principle be raised about $X$ are 'true or false' independently of our being justified in asserting possible answers to the question.

Thus (B) reduces to

(B') Can $P$ ('about $X$') be thought of as being true (or false) independently of our finding ourselves justified in asserting (or rejecting) it?

In considering (B') we must be very careful not to assume an absolute point of view, but we can and must explore this question under the assumption that we are sufficiently justified in asserting that $X$ exists and that the justified assertions are true, which is an assumption about how our acquisitions of justified assertions about $X$ will continue. By a mechanism whose presence we have only inferred and have not yet attempted to explore, noemata provide the basis for formulating all admissible questions about the posited object $X$ and provide the conditions under which 'yes' or 'no' can be rightly answered. But an answer 'yes' under such conditions, while justifying the corresponding assertion, does not yet justify our taking it as a *truth*: that is contingent upon the justifiability of asserting the existence of the considered purported object, which justifiability is a function of the nature of the future accumulation of justified assertions.

The question then is, given a justified assertion which is such that we have convinced ourselves that we are also justified in taking it to be a truth, could it have been the case that the underlying thought was true before we were justified in regarding it as true?

From our considerations above, we can go some way toward this question, by considering the nature of thoughts in the restricted sense of entities for which the question of their truth or falsity arises.

In his *Foundations of arithmetic* Frege argued that the truths of arithmetic are not founded in intuition; they are not justified by appeal to any intuition. In so far as there are truths of arithmetic, they must be true independently of intuition. Thus it is that Frege was driven to a conception of meaning (or of thoughts) in which sentential senses, 'thoughts', are true or false independently of acts of intuition.

Frege was one of the principal exponents of what are now called realist theories of meaning, based upon what Husserl in *FTL* called the concept of 'Absolute Truth' whose extension consists of propositions which are 'truths-in-themselves', that is, their truth is not contingent upon any state of mind or any

*Evidenzen* achieved by us. 'Truth' relativized to such *Evidenzen*, to such inner experiences justifying assertions, Husserl called 'Relative Truth'.

In *FTL* Husserl reached the idea that these two conceptions of truth, far from being alternatives we must choose between, are essentially dependent on each other.

In my sketch above of a criterion for taking a 'justified assertion' (a relative truth) as true, I have provided the basis for an interpretation of Husserl's idea of the mutual dependence of absolute and relative truth, although there are still some steps to take in order to arrive at the full realist notion of truth, at absolute truth, and a phenomenological clarification of its nature in terms of the field of actual and potential appearances. The concept of truth I presented above through the sketched criterion *approximates* to the realist or absolute concept of truth: it makes truth dependent on the perhaps very and typically infinitely distant outcome of the future course of experience and thought. In this respect our emerging conception of truth breaks ranks with the anti-realist conception of truth wherein truth is justified assertability (indeed, this requirement of anti-realism virtually forces a constructivist ontology in which the objects are exactly as they are constructed, so that at any point there is nothing more to discover about the objects considered than what is present to mind). The conception of truth thus far presented as an approximation of the realist or absolute concept of truth also clearly imposes the ideal of the answerability of all questions about a purported object (although *it does not impose the idea of a uniform decision[5] procedure for all questions*). This is clearly a rational idea, for:

*We must be confident that all questions about X could be answered in order to be finally convinced of the existence of X.*

To the extent that we cannot do this, to that extent is our justification for asserting existence weakened. If some question

---

5 e.g. proof and disproof or verification and refutation procedures.

about $X$ is absolutely undecidable by us, then we could not say with perfect justification that $X$ wholly exists, that it is other than a fiction. In such a case $X$ might exist, but we could not be sure of it. That is, what we mean by $X$ (as determined by the relevant noema) is something such that the question $Q$ is a relevant yes-or-no question to ask about $X$; but if we cannot answer $Q$, then we cannot be certain that there is something of the sort that $X$ is (noematically) meant or intended to be (viz. to repeat, something for which $Q$ is a relevant question). But on what grounds could it be even so much as said that $X$ *might* exist even though we are without a proper justification for asserting its existence?

What are the missing steps taking us to an adequate interpretation of the realist or absolute conception of truth in terms of noematic structures, structures present in the field of appearances? We must return once again to the question, If $P$ is justified as a truth, could $P$ have been true independently of our finding ourselves justified in taking $P$ as a truth? That is, what features must a thought have in order for us to be able to construe it consistently and coherently as being true or false independently of our having a justification for taking it to be true or for taking it to be false?

In order to answer this question we must look at and unpack thoughts, the noematic. There is no other way, no way, in short, of avoiding phenomenological analysis. However it must be admitted that a modern realist might well regard our question as bizarre, as forcing an unnecessarily devious route to the obvious, but this is because of the way they (e.g. Frege, Davidson) proceed in the analysis of thoughts. *First*, they employ more or less uncritically the absolute conception of truth, and *second*, things go more or less smoothly for the realist because of an anomaly of speaking.

The absolute concept of truth is embodied in the so-called law of the excluded middle, as a semantic principle which is fully expressed as the conjunction of the following three principles:

The principle of the excluded third:
  There are exactly two truth values: true, false.
The principle of bivalence:
  Every (propositional) thought has at least one of the two
  truth values.
The principle of non-contradiction:
  Every thought has at most one truth value.

Together these principles yield the law of the excluded middle:
  Every (propositional) thought has one, and only one, of the two
  truth values: true, false.

The law of the excluded middle is taken together with the purportedly evident principle (variously utilized),

(T) '$P$' is true if and only if $P$,

where for $P$ we can substitute any sentence expressive of a
propositional thought, as in

'Florence is in Tuscany' is true if and only if Florence is in
Tuscany.

(T) gives us a grip on thoughts via their expression, e.g. as a
means to force out their logical syntax as in its utilization by
Donald Davidson.[6] 'Is true' (having the truth value, true) is
understood under the law of the excluded middle, so that by
working (T) and the law of the excluded middle together one
forces out a logical grammar of the thoughts whereby it is
made manifest how the truth of the whole depends on the
parts of the thought, a part–whole structure articulated by the
logical grammar. (As Frege once said, the principal need for
the concept of truth arises because of the logical imperfection
of our language.)
  There are two features of the law of the excluded middle
which should be attended to. First, it is written in the present
tense, which is to be understood (as in mathematics) as, so to
speak, the eternal tense. Second, it makes no reference to conditions of justifiability. The former and the latter work

6 Donald Davidson, 'Truth and meaning', *Synthese*, vol. 7 (1967), pp. 304–23.

together to force truth to be something which obtains
independently of us as knowing, intuiting subjects. But with
what right does (T) give this conception of truth a genuine grip
on thoughts (which is its principal function)?

There is the appearance of such a right engendered by
speaking, for typically the sentences substituted in (T) make no
mention of justifiability conditions, giving the illusion (as in a
case of thinking being misled by speaking) that the thought
expressed is structured solely by truth-conditions (the truth-
conditional structure of absolute truth, the concept of truth
expressed in classical logic). It is this and virtually this alone
which allows one to regard the realist or absolute conception
of truth, as embodied in the law of the excluded middle, to
have a grip on thoughts. But might it not indeed be a case of
speaking misleading us as to the nature of thoughts? Might it
not be out of expediency that we speak in this way and not that
our thoughts are unstructured by conditions of justifiability
(other than those of mere logical deducibility)?

Indeed, it takes a moment's reflection to realize that there is
much more to the thought that Florence is in Tuscany or, to
vary the example in order to strengthen our point, that it is
snowing in Oslo, than is expressed by the words. Consider:

Is it snowing in Oslo?

Suppose that you are standing in a room of a house in Oslo. If
you were willing to try to answer this question, you would
open the outside door of the house and look around. Even
now, although you are perhaps not in Oslo, you could think of
what kinds of experience you would expect to have in order to
answer this question one way or the other. Indeed, depending
on how you filled in details you could imagine a potentially
infinite range of experiences which if you had them you might
regard as decisively answering the question. The same is true
also of:

Socrates had a small angular scar on his left knee

although it seems that it would be impossible ever to have one of the relevant experiences. That is, there is something about the thoughts which provides such compelling ideas of what experiences would be decisive for the questions. Any adequate account of thoughts must take this aspect of thoughts into account, developing an understanding of its contribution to the whole of the thoughts, which is not to say that all thoughts have such an aspect. Nevertheless the contribution of such an aspect could be such that the concept of absolute truth, the realist concept of truth, fails for the thought. It is in any case clear that without such an aspect, thoughts would be totally incapable of being judged as to their truth, except perhaps through deductive inference.

In no small measure Husserl's *LI* and subsequent writings are concerned with achieving an understanding of this aspect of thoughts. In *LI* Husserl called this aspect of thoughts their 'fulfilment sense'. As he writes in *LI*, Investigation VI, para. 30, a part of each sense

> is an adequate *essentia* which corresponds to it *in specie* in the sphere of objectifying acts whose matter is identical with its own, or, what is the same thing, that it has a fulfilling sense, or that there exists *in specie* a complete intuition whose matter is identical with its own. This 'exists' has here the same ideal sense as in mathematics.

To say that the fulfilment structures are governed by 'an essence' is to say that they are governed by some aspect of relevant noemata.

Indeed, in his *Frege*, Chapter 17 ('Original *Sinn*'), Michael Dummett points out that Frege was not a 'pure realist' because his sentential senses contain or somehow lay out a 'path to their reference', which in this case is either the True or the False. Husserl's notion of fulfilment sense may be regarded as a way of drawing attention to those aspects of senses which might build such a Fregean path.

Husserl observes that there are many variations and degrees in fulfilment senses *vis-à-vis* their adequacy for establishing existence and truth. For geometric propositions, thoughts, the fulfilment senses provide intuitive, perhaps visual, models, but those models are inadequate for truth (a matter to be discussed in later chapters). In the case of objects in the world about us, the fulfilment senses which have to be satisfied for an adequate existence-justifying intuition may very well be infinite.

If a propositional thought is exhausted by its aspect of fulfilling sense, for example by conditions of verification and refutation, then it seems that it can have no purchase on anything beyond what verifies or refutes it. To assert such a thought is then to assert that certain experiences have occurred, so clearly in this case the thought could not be coherently construed as having been true independently of the experience.

This consideration confronts us with the problem of understanding how we can noematically frame objects in such a way that we do not 'mean' or 'intend' the object to be just a certain related set of experiences.

Let us work through an example. (Chapter 3 is devoted to going through two examples in greater detail; the purpose of the present example is to provide clues to be followed up later.)

Consider:

(TW) There is a wall behind me now.

There is something about the thought I am having which is (partially) expressed by (TW) that makes it obvious to me that if I want to verify or refute (TW) I should turn around and look at and perhaps touch what is behind me, looking for something vertical, flat, solid, etc. I do so and experience such a thing. Can I now say that (TW) is true?

It depends on what I intend, on the noema framing 'the wall behind me' as an at least posited object. If I mean by a wall just an occurrence of such experiences, then I can say that (TW) is true. But in fact I find that I mean much more and, indeed, something other than a set of experiences. I find that I mean 'the wall behind me' as something $X$ with much more to it than shows up in such experiences. I mean something with surfaces (I certainly don't mean by 'the wall' a one-sided surface), and with depth, with an interior, and so on. It is not a matter of the meaning of the word 'wall' and whether all of this is built into the meaning of the word; it is a question of how 'the wall' as framed in my thought is to be understood. (When I talk about what I am seeing when looking at 'the wall behind me', I will adjust the elaborateness of my expression to what I sense to be the needs of my hearers to grasp what I mean to be speaking about when I talk of 'the wall behind me'.)

In any case, since this is what I intend, since this is what I mean by 'the wall behind me', before I can say with perfect adequacy and right that it exists and is not just a posited object, I will have to have grasped it in all of its aspects.

Of course, this sounds a bit ridiculous from the point of view of ordinary life. It is sufficient to run painfully into a wall in order to be convinced of its existence. But the conviction here is not the result of a fully rational performance; it does not grow out of a performance of all the observations and considerations which are required if we are to be certain that what is meant or intended exists. From this point of view it is wrong to say that Dr Johnson had refuted Berkeley by kicking a stone, for he simply confirmed the 'common sense' in Berkeley:

*If such minimal sensory contact is all that is needed to affirm the existence of a stone, it is hard to see how there can be more to its existence than such sensory contact.*

For the apparent things in the world about us, given that, as in the case of the wall, they are noematically framed as having much more to them than is seen, felt, etc., existence is certainly not the first, and is properly the *last* thing we know about 'them', although life demands that we make snap judgements and be willing to take the usually not so terrible risks this implies.

But having said all of this, we do not seem to be any closer to understanding the grounds on which, even in the fanciful case that we completed all the tasks necessary in order to be perfectly justified in saying that 'the wall' exists, we could consistently and coherently say that 'the wall' existed independently of our being in a position to be justified in asserting that it exists.

What stands in the way is a problem with which Berkeley confronts us. If properties are completely secured on the basis of, say, perceptions, even though it takes a potentially infinite field of perceptions to secure them fully, we cannot conceive of them as so to speak having a life of their own independently of the securing perceptions, for we cannot (in the spirit of Berkeley's arguments) genuinely think of them as existing apart from perceptions presenting them.

In fact, when in cognitive pursuit of an apparent thing in the world, such as a wall, we at first rely on perceptual properties, describing and building a conception of the wall as a system of parts in terms of such properties. But the more refined our observations and thinking, the more we have to stretch our more or less purely perceptual concepts to the point where we face great difficulties in understanding them in terms of perceptions and perceptual activities. For example, one discovers that the wall is made of a white material. 'White' here is on the verge of not being a strictly perceptual concept. Is the wall white (or colored) throughout its interior? True or false? Is the paint in a can of 'red paint' red only on its surface? We want to answer true to the former and false to the latter. But we quickly become aware of difficulties if we insist that to be colored is to be perceivably colored, for it is hopeless to try to devise a means to affirm this of the wall or the paint. 'Being of such and such a color' has subtly come to refer perhaps to a power of the material to affect light in a certain way, separating it from a direct dependence on the sensory. (An analogous example is discussed in Frege's *Foundations of arithmetic*, para. 26.)

It is the emergence of a concept, of in this case a color concept which is not a sensory concept, which offers to us the possibility of justifying a realism, side-stepping the worries Berkeley presented us with, and so the possibility of forming or constituting propositional thoughts which we can consistently and coherently construe as being true independently of having a justification for regarding them as true. Simultaneously this makes it possible for us to construe posited objects articulated or framed by such concepts as existing independently of our being justified in asserting that they exist.

Now the emergent 'realist' concept 'red' is not unrelated to the correlated 'anti-realist' or sensory concept. The former is, as Husserl would say, founded on or non-independent of the latter, not for matters of truth and existence, but for matters of understanding. Certainly *the* problem we now confront is in understanding this relationship. Even for a concept so seemingly simple as 'red', this is a problem of great difficulty. In order to learn how to begin to solve it, one looks for a simpler situation, and this is provided by elementary mathematics, especially elementary geometry. Some first steps toward an understanding of the relation of 'non-independence' or 'foundedness' (the notion occurs in Husserl's *LI*, Investigation III) will be taken in Chapter 4: first steps toward understanding how in, say, Euclid's Book I, on the basis of intuitive perceptual 'models' (e.g. drawings), one makes a leap to objects which are not sense-perceivable, but the Euclidean figures proper, laying the foundation for a 'realism' with respect to them, or for determining their proper *Seinsinn*.

To recapitulate, we considered two conceptions of 'being real', the first in the sense of being what exists primarily and the second in the sense of what has independent existence. We considered the former first.

A metaphysics of the real in the first sense faces the problem of justifying the existence of what it takes to be real, to exist primarily, and then, the problem of accounting for all other purported objects on this basis. In particular, in so far as they are not reducible to what exists primarily, it has to *deprive* 'them' of existence on rational grounds. In order to give a rational foundation to such a metaphysics it is necessary to achieve a neutral standpoint. We discovered that standpoint in the field of acts of intentional or positional consciousness (which was characterized heuristically as the field of appearances). We arrive at this standpoint by 'bracketing', by regarding what are posited objects as only posited objects (and not as in any way existing objects). Neutrality demands that we find a canonical or uniform criterion which when applied to the field of *positings* tells us when we are justified in asserting that a posited object exists. The criterion should be independent in the sense that from it alone (without applying it) we cannot tell which posited objects will be justifiably taken as existing objects.

Positings are based on formations of thought, on meaning-like entities called noemata, which frame the posited object as this object rather than that object, and which somehow provide a criterion for reasoning about and justifying assertions about the purported or posited objects, the objects so framed. Phenomenology in the strictest sense is the theory of noemata (our understanding will be deepened in subsequent chapters, especially Chapter 3).

Noemata provide conditions of justified assertion, assertions 'about' the purported or posited objects. We formulated a criterion for the justifiability of assertions of existence in terms of the properties of the present and future accumulation of assertions justified in accordance with the criterion implicit in the relevant noemata. We made a distinction between such justified assertions and the justifiability of regarding such assertions *as true* (assertions 'about' square circles might be noematically justified although, because inconsistent, not true; if we did not have a noematically framed criterion of the justifiability of assertions which was independent of truth, we could not have any grounds for 'affirming' contradictory assertions, thereby discovering square circles to be impossible). They are justifiable as true just in case we are justified in regarding the purported objects as existing.

In the last part of the chapter we explored 'being real' in the second sense as what exists independently, finding that a clarification of our right to make such attributions of existence depends on clarifying the peculiar ways in which non-sensory concepts are 'founded' on sensory concepts, proposing that concepts of elementary mathematics are a good place to begin.

The next chapter studies the problem of justifying a realism in our second sense from a different point of view, but with particular reference to mathematics.

# 2

## FROM NAÏVE MATHEMATICAL REALISM
## TO THE ORIGIN OF INTUITION
## AND THE FORMAL

In this chapter I will once again work my way toward phenomenology, toward the theory of noemata, but from a different point of view. This chapter might be regarded as an essay in which some light phenomenological psychology is performed, the purpose being to isolate in some measure the mental phenomena which encourage and feed or sustain an attitude of (naïve) realism which by some accounts is widespread among working mathematicians.

Having more or less isolated some of the principal phenomena which inspire and sustain this attitude, phenomena which we will locate in the nature and function of 'informal meaning' and the intentionality of consciousness (its directedness, its apparent directedness, toward objects), I will again consider how to clarify the sense and justification of this attitude. After isolating the nature and functions of 'informal meaning' as something at work inspiring the attitude of naïve Platonism or realism, I will take a look at the work it does, and once again we will find ourselves encountering noemata as meaning-like entities which nevertheless have a much more complex, powerful, and originating role than can be attributed to linguistic meanings. In particular, a little light will be shed on how these formations of thought, the noemata, provide for and regulate mathematical reasoning and intuition, a light I will try to intensify in Chapter 4.

A mathematician might say readily: 'Infinitely many finite ordinal and cardinal numbers exist. For any finite cardinal number $n$, infinitely many compact, connected $n$-manifolds exist. Transfinite numbers of transfinite cardinal numbers exist.'

What does it mean to ascribe existence in this way? What is the meaning of 'existence' here? What conception of being (what *Seinsinn*) is at work? Nothing cures metaphysical torpor more quickly than vigorous assertions of the existence of infinite totalities, for no sooner does one try to think about these questions of sense than hopes of an answer seem to recede. Infinite totalities cannot depend on us for their existence; if they exist, they must exist independently of our states of mind, of our thoughts, and of the course of our experience. Such reflections seem to deprive us of any understanding of how we could have knowledge of such entities.

Where our understanding fails us so completely, we might be inclined not just to doubt, but to suspect that there is something deeply wrong with assertions that such mathematical objects exist. But what disposes us in some measure to resist this inclination is that mathematicians seem able to direct their minds toward, to think cogently about and accumulate compelling truths about, infinite mathematical entities.

Now, as perhaps Bernard Bolzano was the first to notice, in his *Paradoxes of the infinite*, there seems to be a parity of the following sort between the existence of infinite mathematical entities and states of affairs in the world: they exist independently of us, and this means at least that thoughts 'about them' are true or false independently of our states of mind and of what we happen to know. That is, if infinite totalities exist, they are 'real' in the second sense of Chapter 1.[1] But the problem is to understand how, if they are real, we can know them. An anti-realist conception of the existence of mathematical objects, whereby mathematical objects are mental constructions and, to use a slogan of that arch-anti-realist L. E. J. Brouwer (in his essay 'Consciousness, philosophy, and mathematics'), 'Truth lies only in the past and present

---

1 Henceforth 'real' will be used in this sense, in the sense of 'independent existence'.

experiences of consciousness',[2] *seems* to promise a solution to the problem of mathematical knowledge, but it at least deprives us of having infinite totalities as truly existent objects of thought.
How do we justify a realist attitude toward the existence of mathematical objects?

After arguing that arithmetic could not be founded on 'intuition', 'subjective ideas', etc. in his *Foundations of arithmetic*, Gottlob Frege sought to purge arithmetic thought of any dependence on them. In order to do so, he developed a logic parasitic on a conception of thoughts *qua* propositional senses which are true or false independently of our intuition and knowledge. He was long convinced that 'logic' is the source of mathematical knowledge (save geometry), and at least logic (classical, objectual quantificational logic) frames thoughts as true or false independently of our states of mind. Roughly speaking, what has mathematical existence is to be *read off* from the thoughts shown to be true 'by logic'; such objects would have what we are calling 'real' existence by virtue of the logic. But not a few problems have arisen, seemingly insuperable problems, blocking a conception of 'logic' strong enough to serve as a basis for mathematics.

For example, the principles Frege wrote down turned out to be inconsistent (by an application of Russell's Paradox). It is in any case a very moot point whether there are principles strong enough to 'logically guarantee' the existence of infinitary structures as 'logical'. Principles such as 'axioms of infinity', which say that infinite totalities exist, do not seem to be justifiable as *logical* principles. The incompleteness results of Kurt Gödel for consistent formal systems strong enough to 'contain' certain fragments of arithmetic (Gödel's theorem says that in the language of such a theory there will always be a *true* theorem which cannot be derived in the formal system) make it impossible that any *formal* characterization of 'the logical' be

---

2 L. E. J. Brouwer, 'Consciousness, philosophy and mathematics', in *Collected works I*, ed. A. Heyting (Amsterdam, 1975), p. 488.

sufficient for mathematics. Why is formality necessary? On Frege's analysis, the formal character is essential in order to be certain that mathematical thinking is purged of reliance on intuitive elements, subjective ideas, and the like. It is clear that we must seek a foundation for mathematics outside of logic.

After the failure of his program to derive mathematics from logic (because of Russell's Paradox), Frege tried to construe what he called 'the geometric source of knowledge', a kind of intuitive knowledge (e.g. the intuition of the structure of the complex plane), as the principal source of mathematical knowledge, even to the point of regarding knowledge of the natural numbers as highly derivative and founded on the more immediate knowledge of the complex numbers (much richer than the natural numbers) via the intuition of geometric structures on the Gaussian plane.

The only other even moderately cogent attempt to justify a mathematical realism, this time via a hastily sketched transcendental metaphysics, is due to Gödel in the Supplement to his paper, 'What is Cantor's continuum problem?'[3] Making an analogy between mathematical objects and posited physical entities, Gödel pointed out that there is a form of intuition powerful enough to establish even propositions of transfinite set theory, albeit he pointed with a shaky finger. From Gödel's point of view the presence of such intuitions combined with the act of framing mathematical thoughts in a fragment of the logic Frege isolated, enables one to confer real existence (independent existence) on the posited entities.

In essence the strategy of both Frege and Gödel for developing an understanding of what it would be for at least infinite entities to exist is this: thoughts cast in a realist, interpreted logical syntax together with something somehow having the character of being intrinsically a source of knowledge ('logic', intuition) is sufficient to confer *real* existence on the 'objects' posited in the thoughts secured on the basis of that source.

3 Kurt Gödel, 'What is Cantor's continuum problem?' in *Philosophy of mathematics*, ed. P. Benacerraf and H. Putnam (Englewood Cliffs, N.J., 1964).

We might ask what confers on the considered source of knowledge the right to do this? There are two possibilities here. One is that the only thing that could secure such a right is that the source of knowledge is the medium of some sort of causal relation to the objects. This is not even implicit in Frege and does not seem to be in the back of Gödel's mind either. The other possibility is that, to play on 'logical', all knowledge has fundamentally a 'logical' source in that it is first and foremost *reason* which confers on a 'source' (even perception) the status of knowledge. From *this* point of view a causal account of knowledge, even if it were possible, would be virtually vacuous, for it would be the very last thing we would be able to establish: for physics, physiology, psychology, etc. would have to be finished and unified subjects before the cognitively significant causal chains could be adequately characterized, should any significant fragment of the notion 'causality' survive in future scientific theories.

All of our conferrals of 'reality' would have to have been already performed on grounds other than genuinely established causal connections between physical reality and 'mind'.

This last suggests that there is perhaps a hidden core to the *Sinn* of 'being a real existent' which enables us to establish that purported objects or states of affairs are 'real existents', without having to establish the existence of causal chains between knower and known. Perhaps entities can have 'real existence' without being causally connected to us and yet at the same time we can have sound knowledge of them. It seems that what is above all demanded of us is a clarification of this *Seinsinn* (conception of being), 'real existence'; that the mystery some feel about how we can know infinite mathematical objects if they are 'real' is a result of some measure of *naïveté* here, a *naïveté* which tempts them to think of 'being real' in terms of crude metaphors such as 'to be real is to be out there'.

It seems to be the case that there has not been a cogent and successful attempt to reason to a justification of mathematical realism, an attempt which also explains how we can have knowledge of mathematical objects, especially infinite mathematical objects. If 'being real' is indeed the correct *Seinsinn* for mathematical objects, then, on the basis of a clarification of this *Seinsinn*, seeing how we seem to have knowledge of mathematical objects, including highly infinite objects, we should be able to reason our way to an adequate epistemology. At the same time we must allow that 'being real' is perhaps the wrong interpretation of the being of mathematical objects, or even that there might be mathematical entities falling under different conceptions of being (e.g. real, anti-real). But how do we decide such questions? How do we decide whether or not the proper *Seinsinn* for mathematical objects is 'being real'? If this is the proper *Seinsinn*, and if we knew how to answer this question, then perhaps we could find a way to reason cogently and soundly to a mathematical realism. In his *Cartesian meditations*, Husserl wrote that, 'all wrong interpretations of being come from the naïve blindness to the horizons that join together in determining the *Seinsinne*'. How do we determine such 'horizons'? Where do we look?

An attitude toward mathematical objects as toward 'something real' is not peculiar to a few philosophers or philosophical mathematicians. In his recent 'Some proposals for reviving the philosophy of mathematics', Reuben Hersh claims of 'the typical working mathematician' that 'when he is doing mathematics, he is convinced that he is dealing with an objective reality whose properties he is attempting to determine'.[4] That is, the metaphysical attitude of 'the typical working mathematician' is that of an at least naïve realist. Presumably in doing mathematics it seems to such mathematicians that they are directing their minds toward, thinking about, and discovering truths about independently existing objects. They are naïve realists in the way that most of us are naïve realists about the things we encounter in our day-to-day lives: they seem to be independently existing objects toward which we can direct our minds, about which we can think and discover

---

4 Reuben Hersh, 'Some proposals for reviving the philosophy of mathematics', *Advances in Mathematics*, vol. 31, no. 1 (1979), pp. 31–50.

truths. Hersh cites J. Dieudonné as saying *that each mathematician has the feeling that he is working with something real, although this sensation is probably an illusion, but a 'very convenient illusion'*.

Indeed, it seems that, according to Hersh, when that 'typical working mathematician' is pressed or challenged to give a philosophical account of this reality, he temporarily backs off from this metaphysical attitude, taking refuge in Formalism. If he is diligent, he will even go so far as to formalize some of his work in a suitably rich formal system, suggesting that if it were really convenient to do so, he could in principle carry out his work in such a system. When the irksome philosopher goes away, the mathematician quietly slips back into his attitude of naïve realism.

Now something prompts the attitude of naïve realism in the mathematician. Suppose that this is the wrong attitude, suppose that it confers an incorrect conception of being on mathematical objects. We could explain how this is possible by muttering something about naïve blindness to the horizons which join together to determine the correct conception of being. But this does not encourage us to understand what prompts the attitude and keeps it alive. *How is it that Dieudonné could say that it is probably an illusion, and yet still give in to it?* What is it about this attitude which makes it, as he said, so convenient? How could it be an illusion? What could be the source of its illusoriness (if it is illusory)?

The parity of diverse phenomena sometimes opens the way to truth, such as when Grimaldi, on observing the fringes in the shadow of a hair, was led to the idea that light depends upon a kind of wave motion. But such parity can also be misleading when one is insensitive to differentiae; it can indeed be a source of obfuscating illusion, as in the early theories of vision, a supposed parity between the sun and the eye was allowed to assimilate seeing to shining, or when a certain parity between the space we see around us and the space which is the concern of Euclid's geometry gave people the illusion that in doing geometry they were thinking about worldly space.

We dispel such illusions by distinguishing the confused phenomena, isolating the differences. So it may be that 'the typical working mathematician's' inclination to regard mathematical objects as real is the result of a certain parity between our thinking about mathematical objects and our thinking about the things about us, the distinction which makes an essential difference in their appropriate conception of being emerging only under close scrutiny. It should be noticed that there are several ways in which this confusion, if there is one, might have an effect. First, it might be that the objects of our ordinary experience might be properly called real, but that mathematical objects only seem real because of a certain parity between the way we think and acquire knowledge of the objects about us and mathematical objects. Second, it might be that 'being real' is the correct conception of being for both the objects around us and mathematical objects, but that traits inessential to the *Seinsinn* 'being real' and which the objects in the world about us possess, such as 'being out there' or 'being causally related to us', are mistakenly, even subconsciously, transferred to mathematical objects. At least some need of making such a transfer may be felt even to the point of creating unnecessary problems for our understanding of mathematical objects and of how we can acquire knowledge of them. Perhaps the confusion leads us to ask the wrong questions about mathematical objects (e.g. 'How do they affect our minds so that we can know them?'). Third, it might be that the *Seinsinn* 'being real' is appropriate neither for the objects we encounter in ordinary life nor for mathematical objects. Fourth, it might be that 'being real' is appropriate for mathematical objects, but not for the objects in the world around us, and so on. Of course, it could also be the case that the *Seinsinn* 'being real' is at root incoherent, and so appropriate for nothing.

Let us try now to reach an understanding of what in our experience or consciousness prompts the attitude of naïve realism, and to do this by attempting to fathom Dieudonné's mysterious remark (cited above p. 43) that the 'objective reality' of mathematical objects is probably an illusion, but that the attitude of naïve realism is very convenient. What is convenient about it? The answer to this question will reveal the nature of the parity on whose basis 'worldly being' *qua* 'objective reality') and 'mathematical being' are put on a par. The obvious starting point is to fix on the phenomenon of the 'typical working mathematician' oscillating between Platonism and Formalism. What makes the former more convenient than the latter?

In the spirit of Kurt Gödel's Supplement to 'What is Cantor's continuum problem?', *Formalism* is understood to hold that only *formal meaning*, viz. the use of signs as determined by explicit rules, has a proper and essential role in mathematical thought (for more sophisticated conceptions of Formalism, see Dummett's 'Platonism').[5] One can embroider this idea in various ways, making it less hard-edged, but I think that it is the conception of Formalism which is at issue in Hersh's article and in the quotation from Dieudonné. It is what 'the typical working mathematician' has in mind when he is 'a formalist' on 'philosophical Sundays'.

It is curious that Formalism is contrasted with realism, for the former seems to be a doctrine about mathematical meaning (about the only kind of 'meaning' that has a proper and essential role in mathematical thought), while the latter seems to be a doctrine about existence. The suggestion emerges that when mathematicians are 'naïve realists', they are naïve about the nature and function of another kind of 'meaning' which is at work in their thinking, a kind of 'meaning' which, in the spirit of the discussion in Chapter 1, creates what is the appearance of an objective reality. Then what is 'very convenient' about the attitude of naïve realism is that it is born of a state of mind in which such 'meaning' is given a role. In order to bring this out, let us look at a fragment of a Formalism.

The example I have chosen is a selection of Alfred Tarski's formal axioms for elementary geometry (from 'What is

---

5 Michael Dummett, 'Platonism', in his *Truth and other enigmas* (London, 1978).

46 HUSSERL AND REALISM IN LOGIC

elementary geometry?').[6] I have rewritten them in a way that dramatizes the attitude of informal meaninglessness one is supposed to take toward a formal system in this way heightening our sense of the value of 'informal meaning'.[7] It would be a pointless distraction to describe in detail the formal language and system, so I will not do it (referring the reader to Tarski or to, say, S. C. Kleene's *Introduction to metamathematics* in order to see how such things are done).[8]

Suppose that I write down some signs:

*h, j, k, l, m, p, q, r, s, t, u, w, x, y, z*

Allowing repetitions, these can be formed into infinitely many finite strings, such as

*x*
*szzyzzy*
*pqrllmmmmvk*

and so on.

One now gives mechanical rules which pick out 'the admissible strings' from among all possible finite strings. Then one chooses some admissible strings as 'axioms' and gives mechanical rules for 'deriving' admissible strings from given sets of admissible strings (e.g. the 'axioms'). I shall not bother to give the rules for determining the admissible strings, but the following 'axioms' (I have not given them all) are admissible strings:

(i) *llxyyxmjmyxt*
(ii) *llzuxmkhluzxmkslyqxpmrluyxmkrlzyxmkmuzyxt*
(iii) *llyqxmslzzyxmjmzyxt*
(iv) *llwvpzmjslwuyxmjrluzyxmjmwvuzyxt*

6 Alfred Tarski, 'What is elementary geometry?', in *The philosophy of mathematics*, ed. J. Hintikka (Oxford, 1969).

7 I will be using 'informal meaning' simply to refer to 'meaning' which is *not formal meaning*. Fregean *Sinne* are 'informal meanings'; but our problem here is to discover the nature of 'informal meanings' as they occur in informal or non-formal mathematical thinking.

8 S. C. Kleene, *Introduction to metamathematics* (New York, 1962).

We have the following rule for deriving admissible strings from sets of admissible strings:

if *A* and *B* are admissible strings,
then *A* can be derived from any set containing
*AsB* (an admissible string, where *AsB* will be interpreted below as *B* implies *A*) and *B*.

Suppose that I have given all of the formal axioms (and not only (i)–(iv), which, as we shall see, are four of Tarski's formal axioms, or, rather, can be interpreted in the same way as four of Tarski's can be interpreted) and challenge you to determine whether or not, by reiterated applications of the rule of derivation to the set of axioms or any set formed by adding already derived admissible strings, you can derive the admissible string,

(c) *llyzxmkslzyxmkmzyxt*

This is not a very enticing game.

But consider what happens when I give the following rules for conferring 'informal meanings' on the sign strings:

*x, y, z, u, v, w*, variables ranging over points in space.
*j*, a predicate which when applied to a string of variables *xyzu* results in a string expressing that *x* is as distant from *y* as *z* is from *u*.
*k*, a predicate which when applied to a string of variables *xyz* results in a string expressing that the points *x, y, z* lie on the same straight line and that *y* lies between *x* and *z*.
*l* is understood as (.
*m* is understood as ).
*p* expresses 'not'.
*q* expresses identity of points.
*r* expresses 'and'.
*s* expresses 'implies'.
*t* expresses 'for all . . .'
*h* expresses 'or'.

Reversing each of the strings (i)–(iv) and (c), we have the following translations, interpretations:

(i)   says that, for all points *xyz*, *x* is as far from *y* as *y* is from *x*.
(ii)  says that, for all points *xyzu*, if *y* lies between *x* and *z*, and *y* lies

between $x$ and $u$, and $x$ is different from $y$, then either $z$ lies between $x$ and $u$, or $u$ lies between $x$ and $z$.

(iii) says that, for all points $xyz$, if $x$ is as far from $y$ as $z$ is from $z$, then $x$ and $y$ are identical.

(iv) is left as an exercise in meaning-conferral.

(c) says that, for all points $xyz$, if $y$ is between $x$ and $z$, then $z$ is between $x$ and $y$.

Something powerful has happened. By so conferring meaning we create what is the appearance of objective reference (which may or may not be an illusion). The strings now seem to be assertions *about something*, about points on lines in space, and, more than this, a moment's reflection and we seem to experience 'the truth' of (i)–(iv). Somehow we see that they are true of points (on lines) in space, while we also see that (c) is false. This 'seeing that' is very compelling. Furthermore it might also be the case that the logical axioms (which I did not write down) are experienced as true and that the rule of derivation evidently preserves truth, in which case one can thereby see that (c) cannot be obtained by such transformations from the axioms.

Thus the conferring of meaning creates what is the appearance (which, again, may or may not be an illusion) of genuine objective reference in a way that makes it possible to experience their truth in a manner that may also be illusory but is compelling. This conferral of meaning and the engendered 'truth experience' also enable us to survey the infinity of derivations in the formal system, enabling us to see at a glance that (c) cannot be obtained on the basis of such derivations. Thus it is that the act of conferring meaning on the formal expressions seems to put two sorts of infinite entities within our grasp: the infinite totality of points and lines in space and the infinity of formal derivations.

In their *naïveté*, 'typical working mathematicians' oscillate between Formalism and Platonism (realism). Although it may seem to them that they are oscillating between a view that mathematical entities have objective existence and a view that in mathematics only formal meaning is essential, in the light of our brief discussion above we begin to see that it is *informal* meaning which is responsible for what is the appearance of objective reference and truth, suggesting that mathematicians are really vascillating between the view that only formal meaning has an essential role in mathematical thinking and the utilization of informal meaning. Thus it is that we can see why the attitude of realism is 'convenient': it utilizes informal meaning, which allows one to find one's way around a Formalism.

Let us explore 'informal meaning' a bit more at this naïve level. It is not incompatible with some uses of 'informal meaning' or 'meaning' to say that when Formalism eschews other than formal meaning it is giving up reference to an objective reality. But *what* is it giving up? What is the nature of such reference?

In a naïve attitude in which one seems to focus on mathematical entities on the one hand and formal systems on the other, it might seem that an interpretation of a formal system consists in assigning mathematical entities to the appropriate formal signs. In 'Platonism' Michael Dummett characterized this, too, as a kind of Formalism. From our point of view, this is correct in the sense that informal meaning plays no role, at least no conscious role (we are talking about a naïve state of mind). It seems that all that is at work is 'the mechanism' of pure reference, suggesting the following answer to the question about the nature of reference:

(1) There are formal expressions on the one hand and mathematical entities on the other. Objective reference is obtained by pertinent, pure ('unmediated') correlations of the latter with the former.

This conception of reference underlies the theory of models, where of course it is indeed very convenient.

The principle expressed in (1) poses a serious problem for our understanding. We want to understand how such correlations come about. If we give mathematical entities, say, their names, and do this without mediation, it must be that both formal expressions and mathematical entities are given to us in an unmediated way, and that we can connect and correlate them within the field of their unmediated givenness. There is something which sustains this way of thinking, perhaps simply *naïveté*. As L. E. J. Brouwer wrote (in his dissertation), 'Cantor goes on and talks about his second number class [transfinite numbers] as if he had it before his eyes as a real object.'[9]

Of course (1) is virtually no answer at all unless there are only a finite and small number of mathematical objects and formal expressions. Mathematicians in their realist mode or mood accept the existence of infinitely many natural numbers, 2-manifolds, etc. and it is obviously impossible for them to name them one by one like Borges's Funes the Memorious who, for example, instead of seven thousand thirteen would say *Máximo Pérez*, in place of seven thousand fourteen would say *The Railroad*, other numbers being named *Olimar*, *sulphur*, *the reins*, *the whale*, *the gas*; in place of five hundred he would say *nine*. 'He was, let us not forget,, almost incapable of ideas of a general, Platonic sort.'[10]

In any case, any other way of achieving an infinite correspondence of name and named requires some sort of indirect way of establishing a correlation, some sort of mediation, viz. by 'meanings' understood as intensional entities (what else could there be that does this?), 'informal meanings', but then, of course, 'objective reference' must have a sense other than 'pure reference'. Thus:

(2) There are (informal) meanings that have the power to create and sustain the appearance (which may or may not be an illusion) of references to infinite entities, including perhaps a set of infinitely many names or formal expressions, and of assigning appropriate references.

Recall once more Dieudonné's observation that each mathematician has the feeling that he is working with something real, but that this sensation is probably an illusion. Perhaps indeed what is crucial or at least useful for mathematical

9 L. E. J. Brouwer, 'On the foundations of mathematics' (dissertation), in *Collected works I*, p. 81.

10 From Jorge Luis Borges, 'Funes the Memorious', in *Labyrinths, selected stories and other writings*, ed. D. A. Yates and J. E. Kirby (New York, 1969).

thought is that there are informal meanings which sustain what is the appearance of objective reality and truth. These considerations suggest the following:

(i) In their work, mathematicians find themselves to all appearances thinking about an objective reality and adopt an attitude toward their work which suggests they are investigating an objective reality.

(ii) In their willingness to hide behind Formalism when philosophically challenged to provide a justification of this attitude, they are somehow sensing that the objective reality of mathematical entities is not essential to their enterprise.

(iii) In their unwillingness to retreat from realism permanently, they are sensing that the elements in their thinking which provide what is the appearance of objective reference and truth are in some way essential to that thinking.

(iv) In their reflective *naïveté* mathematicians in some measure fail to notice the role of 'meanings' ('informal meanings') here as a source of what is the appearance of objective reference, objective reality.

(v) Thus when mathematicians resist giving up the idea that mathematics is about an objective reality, what they are resisting giving up (although in their *naïveté* they do not notice this) is the element in their thinking which we have called 'informal meaning'. On the thesis that informal meaning is what above all creates the appearance of objective reality, in resisting giving up the idea that mathematics is about an objective reality, they are resisting giving up informal meaning as having an originative and guiding role in mathematics.

Now of course it is not merely the appearances of objective reference produced by informal meanings which sustain and inspire the realist attitude. Recall our example. On conferring informal meanings on the given formal axioms we had the impression of being able genuinely to *see that* they are true. In the case of the geometric axioms, as opposed to the logical axioms (see Tarski), most of us do this by more or less fully providing ourselves with a picture of a line with points and, in terms of this picture, see what kinds of relations of order are possible. There is something about informal meanings which makes this appeal to intuition available and cogent. This makes it seem as if we are somehow observing mathematical entities (lines and points on lines). The *Evidenz* of the logical axioms, such as the law of the excluded middle, is not so readily explained by a resort to pictures: it is not explained in this way at all. Nevertheless, such laws might be realist in character, conferring on sentential expressions the character of being true or false independently of us, so they will seem to be supported to the extent that we seem to be observing an independently existing objective reality, provided, in the spirit of the discussion toward the end of Chapter 1, ascribed properties are not dependent on, e.g. sensory perception. (This is a matter to be taken up in subsequent chapters.)

It is thus that we are brought to the theme of intuition. There is something about informal meanings which at once creates the appearance of reference to an objective reality and often makes an appeal to 'intuition' available and cogent. This makes it seem as if we are indeed observing independently existing mathematical entities, at least at the present naïve level of consideration. Let me give another example, also from geometry.

Let us consider the problem of characterizing the distance-preserving transformations of the plane, with a view to categorizing them in a significant way. After a little reflection one gets the idea of looking at the actions of such transformations on their own so-called 'traces'. That is, if $A$ is a given point and $T(A)$ the point to which the distance-preserving transformation sends $A$, then the line joining $A$ and $T(A)$, $AT(A)$, is called the trace of $T$ relative to $A$. When $T$ is the identity transformation, $T(A)=A$, there will not be such a line, so let us consider the distance-preserving transformations other than the identity transformation. Now we ask what $T$ does to its own traces, to in particular $AT(A)$. A little reflection yields that there are essentially only three pictures (see Figure 1):

A simple examination reveals that in the first picture $T$ is a reflection, in the second $T$ is a translation, and in the third $T$ is a rotation, thereby categorizing the distance-preserving transformations, putting in our hands some easy theorems, such as: for any distance-preserving transformations performed

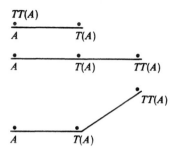

Figure 1    Distance-preserving transformations of the plane

successively, such as a reflection followed by a reflection followed by a rotation, $T$ must be equivalent to either the identity transformation, a reflection, a rotation, or a translation.

One has hereby the illusion of peering into the domain of such transformations, acquiring an insight greatly simplifying what superficially looks like a very complex structure of successively compounded transformations.

But what is 'intuition' and what is its relation to informal meaning? Formalism has been treated as a position to which mathematicians think they can retreat when their realist attitude is challenged. But what makes such a line of retreat available at all? What is the essence of the 'formal' element in mathematical thinking, what does it have to do with the informal element, what do both have to do with intuition, and what do all have to do with 'objective reality'? Let us see if we can locate the peculiarly 'formal' elements.

Consider David Hilbert's opening observation in the Preface of his work with Cohn-Vossen, *Geometry and the imagination*, whose German title is *Anschauliche Geometrie* (meaning 'intuitive geometry'):

In mathematics . . . we find two tendencies. On the one hand, the tendency toward *abstraction* seeks to crystallize the *logical* relations inherent in the maze of material that is being studied, and to correlate the material in a systematic and orderly manner. On the other hand, the tendency toward intuitive understanding fosters a more immediate grasp of the objects one studies, a live rapport with them, so to speak, which stresses the concrete meaning of their relations.[11]

We should try to associate the 'formal' element in mathematical thinking with that which makes possible this crystallization of logical relations. In this spirit we should turn to Frege's seminal 'Begriffsschrift, a formula language, modeled on that of arithmetic, for pure thought'[12] to get some feel for the essence of this element.

That work by Frege was partly inspired by a desire to eliminate completely all reliance on intuition and subjective ideas in constructing and evaluating, say, deductions. Now in fact if one simply looks at the pages of the 'Begriffsschrift', they have the character of presenting a rather beautiful geometry of signs. It would be absurd to say that in exercising the logic presented in that work one was not relying on visual intuition. That point was taken seriously indeed by David Hilbert, who was for a while convinced, or at least hoped, that such geometries of signs contained the very essence of mathematical thinking. (This was in reference to his program of seeking finitary consistency proofs for such geometries of signs, when he tried to show that, just as, say, the trisection of an angle cannot be constructed by a ruler and a compass, so certain signs of contradiction cannot be constructed within certain geometries of signs, e.g. in finitely characterized formal-axiomatic systems for branches of mathematics.)

We cannot say that what characterizes a formal deduction or derivation is that it does not involve intuition, for it is composed of objects of intuition, viz. concrete sign tokens. What characterizes it is that *the use* of those intuitively (e.g. perceptually or even imaginatively) given objects should be completely bound by rules or principles, principles determining which 'geometric' configurations of such expressions can

11 David Hilbert and S. Cohn-Vossen, *Geometry and the imagination* (New York, 1952), p. iii.

12 Gottlob Frege, 'Begriffsschrift', trans. S. Bauer-Mengelberg, in *From Frege to Gödel*, ed. van Heijenoort (Cambridge, Mass., 1981).

count as derivations. It should be completely decidable by those rules or principles whether or not a given configuration is a derivation: if one understands the rules and if one understands how to interpret the relevant perceptual objects, i.e. interpreting them not as physical objects but as tokens of certain specified sign or expression types.

Let us back off a bit and look at the situation in its broadest context:

(1) There is the field of perceptual objects.
(2) We specify a system of signs and of configurations of signs.
(3) This enables us to *interpret* certain perceptual objects as tokens of those sign types and as tokens of those configuration types.
(4) The rules or principles determine which of those configuration tokens can count as derivations, or which sign-configuration types can.

First, there are perceptual objects. A subcategory of these are *interpreted* as sign or sign-configuration tokens of types, interpreted according to definite rules. The perceptual objects become, as Husserl says, 'interpreted objects'. Although the interpreted objects are 'founded' on or (equivalently) 'non-independent' of the perceptual objects, we are only interested in them in so far as they are tokens of specified types. That is, we are not interested in them as 'physical objects' or as tokens of other types, types imposing a different part–whole (or accentuating a different part–whole) structure on the perceptual objects. We are interested in them only in so far as the part–whole structure is imposed on them (an imposition which they furthermore tolerate),[13] by the sign and sign-configuration types we have set out, as is implicitly presented in the characterization of the formal-axiomatic system for elementary geometry which was partially characterized on pp. 46–8 above. A perceptual configuration which can be viewed or construed as having such and such a part–whole structure is a token of a formal derivation. *Checking* a proposed derivation is equivalent to determining whether or not it can be viewed as

---

13 e.g. ///// tolerates an analysis into // followed by ///, but not a red // followed by a blue ///.

having a part–whole structure of the necessary sort, if it is to be an instance of a derivation type.

The perceptual objects (i)–(iv) and (c) above become interpreted as formal expressions. These interpreted objects become *interpreted interpreted* objects when, as we did, we confer informal meaning on them, an informal meaning which they are supposed to express, at least in certain respects, e.g. the way in which the truth of the whole is dependent on the parts, and the ways in which such expressed thoughts are deductively related to other expressed thoughts. The thoughts are by no means completely expressed, for we can relate them to pictures, such as

(P)
$$\overline{\underset{x}{\cdot}\quad\underset{y}{\cdot}\quad\underset{z}{\cdot}}$$

where $x$, $y$, $z$ are distinct points on the same line and $y$ lies between $x$ and $z$. Such pictures are themselves interpreted objects, although no one seems to have spelled out the rules for their use, if indeed univocal and determinate rules can be given.

In connection with the last point, consider (c) on p. 48. (c) is formally refuted by deriving a contradiction from it within the formal system (assuming the formal system has this character). It is intuitively refuted by looking at (P) properly interpreted: it clearly cannot be that if $y$ is between $x$ and $z$ (where the line is interpreted as a 'straight line' and not as, say, part of a circle), then $x$ is between $y$ and $z$. Is this 'seeing that' any less cogent than 'seeing that' such and such a configuration is a derivation of a contradiction from (c)? All that seems to be absent is an explicit laying down of the rules for using interpreted objects of the same ilk as (P).

What is hereby making itself manifest are two ways of reasoning about the objects of elementary geometry, both relying on *interpreted* perceptual objects. The problem of determining the 'truth' of certain thoughts in elementary geometry is reduced to the problem of deciding whether or not there can be certain interpreted objects, e.g. in the one case a derivation token and in the other case a picture.

These considerations suggest the following:

(1) There is something about informal meanings which enables us to choose and interpret objects in such a way that they may be used to secure 'truths' about the entities posited or framed by those informal meanings.
(2) It is by virtue of (1) that we are able to *formalize* mathematical thinking (although of course it is not obvious that all mathematical thinking can be formalized, e.g. thinking with pictures).
(3) But it is also by (1) that we are able to use pictures (as in (P), or as with pictures used to represent the distance-preserving transformations of the plane) to secure 'truths'.

We have noticed a certain, even an obvious parity between (2) and (3): in both cases interpreted objects are used according to explicit or tacit principles (presumably deriving from informal meanings) for reasoning about a mathematical domain.

Intuition is analyzed (plausibly) by Husserl in Investigation VI of *LI* as being based on the use of a particular subcategory of interpreted objects he called 'representing contents of consciousness'. Thus we have to follow some paths opening before us in order to answer the question of the relationship between formal meaning and informal meaning, and the relation of both to intuition. Consider the following:

(IM)

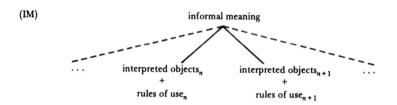

We have many systems $n$,

$$\text{interpreted objects}_n$$
$$+$$
$$\text{rules of use}$$

available for almost any sphere of object positing informal meaning, some systems $n$ corresponding to formalisms, others to 'intuition', but all having the same general form

interpreted objects
+
rules of use

These ideas point toward a way of taking some of the mystery out of intuition (see Investigation VI of *LI*). In the case of arithmetic one can begin to see why 'intuition' is to no avail in securing a foundation: one already has to know the principles of arithmetic before adequate 'interpreted objects' (e.g. numerals) can be instituted.

What we have been calling 'informal meaning' simply falls within the Husserlian 'noematic' (as discussed in Chapter 1). We must now attempt to understand how the noematic provides the foundation for reasoning about its purported objects (or objects posited on its basis), how, in short, it provides

interpreted objects
+
rules of use

These matters will be explored in Chapters 3 and 4, with a return to ontological problems in Chapter 5.

# 3

## NOEMATIC ANALYSIS

In this chapter we will be concerned with the analysis of noemata structuring acts of cognizance and consciousness in which an object is posited. Such acts engage a noema or in particular a noematic sense which give to the act the character of positing *this* object rather than *that* object. As Husserl says, the noematic sense provides 'the what'. Our task here is to become familiar with these formations of thought, the noematic senses, which constitute the proper object of phenomenological inquiry, and I propose to gain this familiarity by studying two examples.

Noemata are not hypothetical entities, not mere theoretical entities dreamt up for their explanatory power. Rather they are entities on which we can reflect: they are themselves formations of thinking and so they are *intelligible* objects; we furthermore learn about them by reflection, reflection of the sort I shall illustrate below.

It must be emphasized that I am focusing on only one aspect of noemata which in general are of a very complex nature. I am focusing on that core of object-framing noemata called the 'noematic sense' on which other and perhaps modifying parts of fuller noemata are founded. As will become clear, although I agree with some writers, such as McIntyre and Smith,[1] that it is at least heuristically useful to think of noematic senses as analogues of Fregean senses for singular

1 R. McIntyre and D. Smith, 'Husserl's identification of meaning and noema', *The Monist*, vol. 59 (1975), pp. 115–33; 'Intentionality via intensions', *Journal of Philosophy*, vol. 68 (1971), pp. 541–61; and also Dagfinn Føllesdal, 'Phenomenology for analytic philosophers', in *Philosophy in Scandinavia*, ed. R. Olsen and A. Paul (Baltimore, Md., 1972).

terms, I greatly disagree with their strong assimilation of noematic senses to such senses and in particular to the thesis that noematic senses are adequately expressible by sets of descriptions framing an object. Our noematic analyses will show that this is not the case. Such an account of noematic senses could not in any case provide a foundation for the principles of reasoning about purported objects. In particular, it could not provide a foundation for the use of interpreted objects, in the sense of the last chapter, the use which, for example, founds 'intuitions of' posited objects (when the interpreted objects are of a special sort which Husserl called 'representing contents' in *LI*). McIntyre and Smith write as if Husserl imposed a theory of meaning on acts of consciousness, viz. by arguing that Husserl in effect extended Frege's theory of senses to all kinds of mental acts. But what must be emphasized is that the study and analysis of noemata, the discovery of their nature and structure, constitutes phenomenology.

In doing phenomenology one turns to episodes of intentional consciousness, of directed consciousness. It becomes apparent that such episodes are directed toward definite objects, to this object rather than that object, by something. To such entities one gives a name, perhaps a suggestive one, such as 'noemata'.[2] Now the problem is to determine their nature by reflection, by actually looking and seeing what they are like, and to do so as much as possible without presuppositions: without, for example, presupposing that they are linguistic meanings and thereby perhaps concealing aspects which may otherwise have been noticed, aspects perhaps deeply important for our understanding. In particular one must be careful to avoid importing any of the metaphysical presumptions discussed in the Introduction. After all, Fregean senses are capable of forming sentential senses which have objective truth values. Whether or not there are such senses is exactly what is most problematic.

Let us turn to the examples.

2 From the Greek, meaning (given a philosophical interpretation), 'what is thought'.

Figure 2    Frazer spirals

### THE FRAZER SPIRALS (EXAMPLE 1)

Consider Figure 2. 'The Frazer spirals' is the name of an optical illusion effected by looking at a drawing of certain grey and white banded 'twisted ropes' in the form of concentric circles placed against a background which heightens and strengthens the illusion of seeing 'spirals' and not concentric circles. The illusion is powerful and persistent: it is sustained through repeated and long-term viewings, and it takes a steady hand and eye to trace the circles in a way that avoids shifting from one circle to another thereby continuing the deception.

The purpose of the present exercise is to study the

relationship between 'the illusory spirals'[3] and 'the drawn concentric circles'. We shall be interested in the relationship between the noemata framing the respective purported objects and not in their physical–physiological relationship (supposing that it is coherent to speak of that). We appear to have some right to suppose that there are two different noemata to compare because it seems as if we can speak of two different observations, one of the illusory spirals and the other of the concentric circles (despite one's *not* being able *not* to have a visual experience of spirals).

We should also like to determine in what sense the respective posited objects of the perceptions are objects. There are two special points of interest here. The first has to do with so-called causal accounts of perception in their use in attempts to ground realist theories of perception. Such a use would attempt to make sense of the claim that what one is really perceiving on the paper is a drawing of concentric circles and not spirals by positing a physical–physiological causal chain between perception and paper. We shall find that the question of what is 'really' drawn on the paper is not at all answered by an appeal to a causal chain. Since in this case there is no need to establish a causal relationship between perception and perceived in order to secure knowledge of 'what is *really* there', the possibility emerges of one being able to think coherently and consistently of mathematical objects as 'being real' without there being such a relationship.

Another point of interest has to do with understanding the relationship between phenomenal or, say, visually experienced objects and infinite mathematical objects, such as the relationship between drawn triangles and Euclidean triangles (using 'infinite' in the spirit of David Hilbert), a matter to be discussed in the next chapter. Indeed, the following analogy suggests itself:

$$\frac{\text{Frazer spirals}}{\text{concentric circles}} = \frac{\text{drawn triangles}}{\text{Euclidean triangles}} = \frac{\text{something visible}}{\text{something invisible}}$$

3 Whenever I mention 'spirals' it will be the purported 'twisted rope' spirals that I have in mind.

This analogy prepares the way for understanding more fully how, in the spirit of the end of the last chapter, drawn triangles can be used as 'intuitive models' for, and for reasoning about, Euclidean triangles. (The analogy is of course very rough.)

It is probably worth emphasizing the anti-reductive character of the phenomenological outlook: in the case of the Frazer spirals, it will be quite wrong to regard them as 'illusory objects'. In some measure they are objects in their own right. I say 'in some measure' because they will prove to be defective in some ways. Our very impulse to call them 'defective' makes manifest the association of an ideal of a kind of perfection with objectuality, an ideal whose significance we might well ponder (cf. Kant's analogous meditations in Book II of the Transcendental Dialectic in the *Critique of pure reason*).[4] We might wonder whether *any* purported or posited object can live up to the ideal.

Let us now turn to the example. I will begin at a very superficial level, covering the same ground many times, but with increasing phenomenological insight. Indeed, the full phenomenology of even a single such example is a vast undertaking, new problems arising at each stage. My aim here is only that of proceeding far enough to gain some familiarity with the fundamental structures which begin to emerge, learning something of significance about noemata, something which will show through despite the incompleteness and imperfections of the investigation (e.g. in introducing the notion 'fragment of the visual field', something itself in need of a more thorough clarification).

If I now look at Figure 2, I see that I do indeed experience spirals, but in tracing them with my finger I discover not spirals but rather concentric circles. Thus there are in effect two perceptual experiences, one an experience of spirals, and the other an experience of concentric circles. But this clumsy observation obscures too much. Let us do better.

---

4 Immanuel Kant, *Critique of pure reason*, trans. Norman Kemp Smith (New York, 1963), p. 488, A572/B600.

I look at Figure 2 and ask myself what I am seeing. Consider:

If I mean to be attending to what is drawn on the page, then the proper answer is that I am seeing concentric circles, even if they are not visually apparent. If I answer that I am seeing spirals but mean to be attending to what is drawn on the paper, then I have answered incorrectly. But if I mean to be attending to what I am visually experiencing as I am visually experiencing it, to my 'visual impression', then it would be incorrect to say that I am seeing concentric circles, but correct to say that I am seeing spirals.

This description is based on a naïve, commonsensical understanding of perceptual experience. We eliminate this *naïveté* and produce a more refined understanding by attending to the respective noemata, roughly, to what in each case 'I mean to be seeing'.

Let us consider first the circumstance where what I mean or intend to be attending to is 'what is drawn on the paper before me', but let us suppose that I have not yet determined fully what is drawn there, viz. that concentric circles are. Perhaps a discomfort in eye or the context of presentation of the picture (e.g. in a chapter in a book labelled 'Illusions') suggests to me that perhaps spirals are not drawn there.

Certainly in such a case the noematic sense or, for short, noema (I will take this liberty), is partially expressed by 'what is drawn on the paper before me'. Now there are lines, shapes, shaded figures, and much else that is present in my visual field, including spirals. I am suspicious of the spirals, but I construe part of what I am experiencing as a piece of paper and as a piece of paper lying in a certain relation to myself, just as I construe other shapes as being parts of my body such as 'my hand' and perhaps 'my hand raised for finger tracing of lines on the paper'. I also construe some of the things I see, certain parts of lines or line parts as on the paper, even though I withhold such a positional or affirming interpretation from certain lines of which those parts seem to be parts, viz. 'the spirals', as being on the paper. All of these conferrals are, as Husserl says, 'partial intentions' whose noemata are woven together into the full noema framing the piece of paper with the drawing as part of my immediate, perceived environment.

Let us go through this description again, but in a more refined way. I have introduced the notion of my perceptual field and the idea of construing fragments of it as this or that. This suggests that there is something available to me which is as it were unconstrued which I can behold freely, some pure givens which I can take to be a giving of this or that. Let us try to clarify this idea. Consider:

cat

A speaker and reader of English will instantly see here a word in the English language with a quite definite meaning. It is indeed impossible to experience this directly as one would who knew nothing of the alphabet and nothing of written English.

Consider another example. Suppose that you are given a novel of which you know nothing. You read one of the later pages. The experience you have of this page you would be completely incapable of having if you read the page immediately after reading up to it (thoughtfully), from the beginning of the novel, for then the page will function as a virtually transparent window showing you more of the world the novelist has created, an exhibition you will not be able to avoid. In these cases a background of sense or thought is so to speak instantly engaged, somehow unavoidably engaged, from which we cannot free ourselves. Thus it is with perception. Almost every perception has the character of being a perception of 'something there in the environment'. Just as in reading a novel there is somehow generated a field of thought, in some way present and active, even though not fully and explicitly in our awareness, a field which works to produce a smooth, easy, and unreflective understanding of the next page as it read, so in a comparable way, there is a background of thought, something noematic, which is continuously giving a sense to our perceptual experience.

What then can we mean by 'perceptual field'? Some uninterpreted field of neutral stuff? *Only* if we can be sure that it is not a hypothetical construct. I close my eyes and open them and I cannot make myself not see there before me 'a shelf of books'. I can describe again what I am seeing in an abstract and neutral vocabulary of shape and color but I cannot free myself from the awareness of there being a shelf of books before me, any more than when I look at

cat

I can free myself from the awareness of the presence of the word 'cat', or any more than I can, when reading a novel, free myself from having read all that went before when I read the next page immediately after having read all that went before. I can think, well perhaps it is not a shelf of books, but a shelf of boxes which have been made to look like books, or perhaps it is not a shelf at all but a cunning picture of a shelf designed to fool the eye. Or recalling tricks done with perspective I can think that perhaps it is not a shelf of objects at right angles to my sight, but something at a highly oblique angle (as in anamorphic art) which, due to misleading cues as to depth, and so on, looks like an array perpendicular to my line of sight. And so on, virtually *ad infinitum*, seemingly varying over the same 'perception', pointing to an uninterpreted stratum over which the interpretations may vary, on which different noematic senses can be conferred. Thus such reflection seems to point to a field, a pure or uninterpreted but infinitely interpretable sense-perceptual field, whose integration with interpretive noemata produces experiences having the character of being perceptions of things in one's environment. Not only Husserl but psychologists of perception have tried in various ways to take this field as a genuine entity; in his *ID* Husserl tried to characterize it in the weakest possible way as the difference between a filled and an empty perceptual noema ('hyletic data'), as, e.g. that which makes the difference between merely thinking 'the moon over the mountains' and seeing the moon over the mountains, or at least seeming to do so. As I will shortly explain, we need not concern ourselves with the question of such a pure uninterpreted component of perceptual experience. But what these considerations suggest is that a perception as an object on which we reflect (while we are having it or in retrospect) may be understood as having two parts, viz. (i) a noematic nucleus which may be varied and through which the perception has the sense of being a perception of a purported object $X$, and (ii) invariable components having the abstractive sense, 'being a *presentation (Vorstellung)* of a part of $Y$' or 'being a presentation of such and such a part of $Y$',[5] any of which we are free to accept or reject. The $X$ may or may not be meant to be the $Y$. The second category of parts of a perception are what Husserl called in *LI* the 'representing contents' of the perception or, to use the generic term, 'interpreted objects'. They are given as 'partial intentions'. They are 'interpreted' by the full noematic sense of the perception (which I have characterized as the first part and which may be varied), specifying determinately the 'such and such' and the $Y$. The beauty of this analysis is that we do not need to posit an underlying uninterpreted stratum in our perceptual experience in order to understand how we can re-evaluate a perception; the assumption is that any perception can be and is, in the natural course of thinking experience, broken down into such partial intentions which may be interpreted or woven together in a new way through the instituting of an altered overarching noematic sense.

Let us return to our example in order to illustrate these ideas. Now it is obvious that while our perceptions are directed toward objects (such as the sun or the sun setting), the objects are not isolated. Our perceptions are of objects-in-environments, so that the noematic sense of a perception frames not just an object, but an object-in-an-environment.[6] It is this, for example, which puts them into a definite relation to ourselves *qua* beings in the same environment or world.

5 These phrases express ideas which can be expressed in different grammatical forms (cf. the illustration (E) on p. 68).

6 This emphasis was inspired by Husserl's later writings, especially his *Crisis of the European sciences and transcendental phenomenology*, trans. David Carr (Evanston, Ill., 1970).

I find that my perception of the page with the drawing producing the illusion of the Frazer spirals can be analyzed into
the following 'partial intentions' or 'partial perceptions',
assuming that I am taken in by the illusion:

(E) a presentation of my left arm (*qua* part of my environment)
a presentation of my left hand
a presentation of a table top before me
a presentation of a piece of paper on the table before me
a presentation of a piece of paper which I can reach out and
touch with my left hand
a presentation of lines on the piece of paper
a presentation of shaded areas on the paper
a presentation of the colors of this and that part of the paper
a presentation of a drawing of spirals on the paper

Before going on there is a matter of some delicacy to discuss. Consider again looking at

cat

or reading the next page in a novel after reading all that went
before. In such cases I may not express to myself what I am
experiencing, e.g. that I am seeing the word 'cat' or that such
and such characters with such and such personalities and
quirks in such and such a situation are given, but I can more or
less do so on reflection on what is in effect the noematic background. The list (E) is of such a nature; it seems to me to bring
out the noematic background, and it is not the result of an
explicit judgement on my part, but one which comes to me as
somehow 'prejudged'. But how rich is this noematic background? In producing a list (such as (E)) when is it that I am
simply drawing out this background; and when is it that I am
making new judgements, adding new elements of interpretation to the already interpreted or representing contents,
thereby modifying the initial perception, making it richer,
rather than reporting on it?

I do not think that we can provide a criterion for deciding
such questions, and it does not seem to be essential that we be
able to do so, since what interests us is so to speak the invariant
structure of perceptual noemata; the accidental modification

of a perceptual noemata of the sort just mentioned will not affect this invariant structure. Perception is after all dynamic.

There are, however, clear cases where there is no question that we are developing our perception, as when we try to articulate conceptually features of what has the character of being presented in a partial intention, in a partial perception. For example, we might be presented with a drawing of a shape for which we have no words characterizing that particular shape, or we might notice two different shades of red for which we have no words specifically differentiating them. In contrast, once we have and have fully mastered such concepts they might be assimilated into the noematic background (as Husserl might have said, *Bedeutung* or 'conceptual meaning'[7] gets assimilated into noematic sense), modifying it, enabling us to *re-cognize* the colors or shapes without having to draw out or make explicit to ourselves the assimilated concepts, just as a mathematician who is expert in group theory can recognize a structure (say, a finite simple group) and begin reasoning coherently about it as if it were one, even though it might not have been given as this, without having to rehearse the definition and fundamental theorems. I will in any case assume that the noemata I am studying are in this sense *conceptually rich enough* to sustain the expressions (E) as expressing aspects of the full noema at issue. (It is in some measure obvious that this phenomenon of assimilated concepts underlies what is sometimes referred to as 'the theory-ladenness' of perception.)

With all of these considerations in mind, let us continue with the example, going through the stages in which the illusion of the Frazer spirals is found to be an illusion and more particularly determining in what sense the visually experienced 'spirals' are objects.

Instead of using 'sense' I will often say 'has the sense of being an *X*'; for 'partial intention' or 'partial perception' I will say, 'fragment of the perceptual field' ((E) illustrates this).

Presuming adequate conceptual richness of the noema, the

7 *Bedeutung* is therefore not to be confused with Frege's use of the word. 'Assimilation' corresponds to what Husserl in later writings referred to as 'sedimentation'.

objects purportedly presented in the fragments (E) of my perceptual field also have the sense of being related to one another in various ways; there are fragments of the perceptual field which have the sense of being presentations of these relationships:

a presentation of my left hand above the table top to the left of the piece of paper with the drawing,
a presentation of a piece of paper before my eyes,
a presentation of this line part connected to that line part,

and so on. Some such relationships were already mentioned under (E), such as lines 'on' the paper. Furthermore, the fragment of my perceptual field with the sense of being a presentation of my hand is further presented as being something I can move, as having a finger I can raise, the finger being such that I can use it to trace lines on the paper by following and guiding my finger with my eye (so to speak), and so on and on.

Consider now:

(Cir) There are circles drawn on the paper, not spirals.

How can I reason my way to a decision about the truth of (Cir)? My ability to do so rests on the full noematic background; that background merged with the thought expressed by (Cir) regulates what I must or can do in order to decide (Cir).

The first thing to notice about (Cir) is that we have to work in order to find a way of verifying it. We *understand* (Cir) and then in terms of the array of woven-together fragments of our perceptual field we work out ways in which, in this setting, we could carry out performances whose success would yield that (Cir) is true. We cannot say that the thought expressed by (Cir) has all such possibilities built into it, that it comes to us with verification or refutation conditions built into it. Certainly, for example, Michael Dummett in his anti-realist interpretation of thoughts often speaks as if they do have such conditions, that in fact they are exhausted by such conditions. But it is reflection on the full noema framing the paper with the drawing in such and such an environment which must be drawn upon and thought through in order to bring out ways of deciding (Cir); this reflection is nothing other than the process by which we achieve a fuller understanding of what is posited as being this paper and its environment, an understanding essential for finding ways of deciding (Cir). It is the full noematic background framing this object in this environment which regulates the possibilities of deciding (Cir) together, of course, with an understanding of (Cir).

That some of us see instantly how to go about performing the verification or refutation certainly creates the illusion that what in this situation could count as verifying or refuting it is immediately a part of the thought itself; but this immediacy is an illusion produced by that phenomenon of mind discussed earlier which enables us to understand immediately the hundredth page of a novel after reading all the pages up to that page without having to rehearse or otherwise bring explicitly to mind all that is relevant that has happened before in the novel. Such blindness to the deep and complex noematic field underlying even the simplest acts of verification, the field which gives those acts sense, has misled the whole empiricist tradition. The vast project of bringing to explicitness such noematic fields is a necessary condition for the evaluation and justification of any empiricism.

But let us continue. Our task is to re-evaluate the fragment:

a presentation of spirals on the paper

While accepting the interpretations of all other fragments, we call this interpretation into question.

Easy reflections on the nature of circles show us that such things are closed curves; that one can get from any one part back to the same part by tracing and without ever leaving the figure, moving in one direction only. This is not true of spirals. (This very statement itself can be greatly clarified.) Thus one test to see whether or not 'being a presentation of spirals on the paper' deserves our final approbation is to place my finger on a part of the purported spirals and trace; if I come around to the same part, then indeed I must conclude that the perceptual fragment 'being a presentation of spirals on the paper' is illusory. Or I could take a piece of cardboard and cut out circles of various sizes and place them on the drawing and see if they can be made to outline circles where there seem to be spirals. Or I could use any manner of compass rather than finger tracing. And so on indefinitely.

All of these possible performances are justified in terms of the background noema, the sense they are given through that noema. The subsequent perceptual performances of any of these activities are themselves given as fragments of my perceptual field.

So I perform the finger tracing and find that I can no longer accept that the perceptual fragment with the sense of being a presentation of spirals drawn on the paper can justify the assertion that there are spirals drawn on the paper, and furthermore discover by using cut-out circles that there are circles drawn there.

The noematic sense provides a sense for, or 'interprets' (makes 'interpreted objects' of), the already given and (as a result of my performances) new fragments of my (dynamic) perceptual field which works to throw out the fragment with the sense of being a presentation of spirals drawn on the paper. An understanding of the noema provided the means for using these fragments to reason about what is present on the paper (these perceptual fragments play the role of 'interpreted objects' in the paradigm presented and briefly discussed at the end of Chapter 2). We shall next study an example which is somewhat more revealing about the nature of noematic senses and how they regulate the use of 'perceptual fragments' to reason about 'perceptually presented objects'.

But what becomes of the perceptual fragment with the sense of being a presentation of spirals drawn on the paper? We cannot accept it as telling us something about the paper. But what about 'the spirals'?

All fragments of my perceptual field are present with the same value as having the sense of being a presentation of such and such. Each can be re-evaluated. What prevents us from preserving the perceptual fragment with the sense of being a presentation of spirals on a piece of paper and throwing out all other fragments in conflict with it (i.e. refusing to allow them to be used to justify assertions)? Do we have a free choice? Can we begin with this fragment and build up a world distinct from the world which excluded it? Some forms of empiricism would allow us to do exactly this, but precisely because they overlook the full noematic sense whereby the spirals are on a piece of paper in my environment which is capable of being acted on in various ways.

Nevertheless I can take a so to speak smaller fragment of my perceptual field, that which has the sense of being a presentation of spirals, and reinterpret it, as I can always reinterpret perceptual fragments, so that no sense is given to it which would put it into conflict with fragments of my perceptual field having the sense of being presentations of parts of the world I am in. This transformation of noema also carries with it new conditions for reasoning about 'the spirals', e.g. fragments of my perceptual field produced by observations of finger tracing and the like can no longer be used to discover truths about the spirals. They are no longer posited or understood as being objects which can be acted on and investigated in this way.

*How can we reason about the spirals?*

We cannot trace them with our eyes. This loses the spirals. We are using the concept 'spirals'. Therefore we should be able to count them and to determine, for example, what their global properties are and what the relationship between their local and global properties is. But in trying to do this without at the same time using operations such as tracing or pointing which would imply that they belong to the world in which we are physically active, a world in which they do not exist, we find that we are deprived of any means of deciding how many there are or what their geometric properties are (try to count them, or if, as some do, you seem to see only one spiral, try to verify without using such a procedure that there is only one spiral). Thus the ordinary concept 'spiral' is completely inappropriate. At best we can call the character of what is presented to us 'spiral-like'. We find that we are left with a noematic sense which as far as the spirals are concerned is conceptually very poor; at best the noematic sense functions to construe 'the spirals' as what has the character of being presented in a perceptual fragment produced by looking at such and such a drawing. This is the sense of 'the Frazer spirals', together with aspects of the sense which limit how it can be reasoned about, so that 'the spirals' are not put into an environment where 'the spirals' as objects are lost because they are in deep conflict with it.

In some measure we have the spirals as objects, but we seem to be deprived of any power to think about them (I mean about them as they present themselves, and not as, e.g. an optical illusion, an illusion to be explained, as given in an experience produced by such and such a means under such and such circumstances), for there do not seem to be any legitimate questions we can ask about them, e.g. about their number, about their geometric properties, and so on. We do not have available a realm of concepts which would be appropriate, e.g. concepts of somehow fuzzy or inexact numbers of an appropriate sort, or concepts of curves whose global properties are not regulated by their local properties, or vice versa. Perhaps with some serious thinking we could reach an understanding productive of such a deviant mathematics.[8] But in any case we have produced a challenge to our imagination, and with the observation of our right to have 'the Frazer spirals' as potential objects, the possibility of being able to enter a new and bizarre world. I say 'potential objects' exactly because we have no clue as to how to think and reason about

---

8 We thus encounter here a variation of what Husserl in his *Crisis* called 'the problem of the mathematicization of the plenum', but here the mathematics is not ready-made.

them further: there seems to be more to 'them' than we know how to grasp. What we have been given in perceptual experience stands before us as something to be interpreted, as something on which we might hope to confer a meaning which will have what properties? The best we can say is that the noematic sense will provide us with principles for reasoning about such 'spirals' and so at the same time present us with a set of concepts framing the questions to be answered, presumably by utilizing the perceptual fragment presenting 'the spirals' in some way, a way which does not implicitly put 'the spirals' into some domain with which they are incompatible, as in our environment, where we can trace lines.

In the next chapter we shall encounter some serious proposals for a new mathematics emerging from situations produced by means analogous to this one. Furthermore we shall notice in our considerations of Euclid's Book I that it seems that drawn geometric figures, because of their 'imperfections', cannot be strongly reasoned about; and that the Euclidean figures come closest in some sense to the objects one can reason about.

This discussion has prepared the way for a discussion of some problems to be undertaken in the next example, problems connected with the meaning of a very powerful principle Husserl enunciated in *FTL*, viz. that categories of objectuality and reason (*Evidenz*) are correlated with one another. I restated this principle in the Introduction as

*no entity (for us) antecedently to a way of thinking and to thinking in that way*

### THE DOG IN THE FOG (EXAMPLE 2)

In acts of consciousness we posit this object rather than that object by virtue of a noematic sense; in the cases we will be concerned with, the noematic sense frames the object as such and such a determinable $X$ (cf. Husserl's *ID*, para. 131) in such and such an environment (or 'world'). If we bring such senses to expression, what do we find? Do we find at least a set of descriptions describing the object itself? This was not the case for 'the Frazer spirals'. At best they were identified in terms of a situation which evokes the illusion. Providing any kind of adequate, sufficiently identifying description of the experienced spirals, the determinable $X$ in this case was a problem of considerable difficulty, one requiring a clever and imaginative artificer of hitherto unformed concepts, assuming that such are indeed possible. (Such conceptually recalcitrant phenomena are not really unfamiliar, e.g. the smell of coffee, although there are genuine logical difficulties attending the formation of concepts adequate for thinking about Frazer spirals.) The best we seem to be able to do is hold 'the spirals' in mind; they seem to throw off any means we have at hand for determining their properties, for making our grasp of them more determinate.

Let us look at a less recalcitrant example. I am walking through a thick fog along the Suffolk coast one afternoon. I see before me a shape in the fog. My perception has the sense of being a presentation of something there in the fog. It could be far away and huge or close and small. It might be nothing at all but a thickening of the fog in a certain direction or even some fairly amorphous eidetic image my eyes are projecting into the fog.

These considerations represent possible reinterpretations and so transformations of my current perception. But my perception does have the sense of being a presentation of something $X$ there in the fog, some thing $X$. The noematic sense, in as much as it yields descriptions of the purported $X$, is extremely impoverished, for no particular shape or color or other quality can be attributed to it.

Nevertheless the noematic sense is rich in other ways: it posits the $X$ as being in my environment located in a certain direction from me and having some rough boundaries marked out in the fog, though with little clue as to their dimensions.

How can I bring the determinable $X$ to a greater degree of determination? It is in effect by reflection on the aspects of the noematic sense which places the purported objects in an environment, an environment in which I can act, which provides me with an understanding of how to bring it to further determination. Thus, for example, I walk forward, trying to get closer, taking a closer look, perhaps reaching out to feel the object, and so on. I do so and discover that there is a dog there.

All of the activities I perform acquire a sense determining the relationship with the determinable $X$, a sense founded on the initially given noematic sense.

An array of acts of consciousness which are in certain ways continuous with one another is produced and they all have the character of being presentative of aspects of my own activity and my environment having a bearing on determining further the determinable $X$, ultimately all forcing the conclusion that there was a dog standing before me in the fog. When I have encountered the dog and have seen it much more clearly, the expanded noematic sense now functions in the same way to enable me to go on and make further observations about the dog, e.g. whether or not it is friendly, what breed it is, what color its fur is, and so on.

The important feature of the example is this: I want to say that although initially the $X$ was not fixed by the sense of a set of descriptions of it, it was fixed as an object which could be reasoned about in a certain way. The noematic sense fixed the object in this way. That is, it was fixed as something which is such that certain episodes of consciousness (e.g. observations) produced in certain ways could be used to justify certain assertions about the posited but initially virtually indeterminate $X$. The noematic sense contains (as a kind of core) principles determining what fragments of the perceptual field can count and, in what way, as *Evidenzen* founding justified assertions about the initially posited $X$. Notice that had I initially taken the shape to be a child, these principles would have provided me with the means of correcting my error.

If on the other hand the attempts at further determination came to nothing, one might try reinterpreting the initial perception as, e.g. being a projection of an eidetic image. Then the determinable $X$ is of a quite different character: it is not posited as being part of my environment. In order to make it more fully determinate, entirely different 'principles of reason' would have to be utilized prohibiting the object $X$ from being reasoned about in the same way as objects in my environment, and thereby placing it in a different world. Perhaps in this case it could be 'reasoned about' (that is, and this always means, its properties or characteristics could be subject to justified assertion) on a different basis within the full field of past, actual, future, and potential acts of consciousness according perhaps to quite different principles.

In these examples we begin to get a feel for the sense in which the noematic background, and in particular a noematic sense framing an object $X$, provides the principles of reasoning by which a special category of 'objects' (interpreted objects, representing contents) is used to secure at least justified assertions and, in the long run (see Chapter 1), truths about $X$. In these examples the 'interpreted objects' were fragments of our perceptual field having the interpreting character of being produced in a certain context with certain ends in mind (e.g. the string of perceptions having the sense 'produced by observing finger tracing'). We have also seen how some objects $X$ (e.g. the illusory spirals) may sustain little or no thinking or reasoning because of the poverty of adequate concepts.

These examples begin to give us a feel for the noematic structures and how they act to regulate reasoning and how it is that the way in which one reasons about an object places it in a particular world; how, in short, a way of reasoning is constitutive of a world. There is much that is vague, of course, but the vagueness is of the sort that can be eliminated by going on, by performing ever more complete phenomenological analyses, continuing as we have begun. We should then be able to arrive at an understanding of the mutual dependence of noematic *Sinne*, principles of reasoning, and conceptual systems, and how they work together to give us access to, to constitute, worlds. In our contemplation of the Frazer spirals we began to have some intimation of the promise of phenomenological investigation to provide the means of liberating the imagination and finding ways into regions of objectuality which must seem to us now bizarre, but which may greatly increase the dimensions of our being, and of our capacities for thought. But there is only the vaguest hint of such a promise. To follow the hint, we must learn how to gain increasing power over the vast noematic structures which shape and limit our thinking. To accomplish this, we must begin in a far simpler situation than those discussed in this chapter: for example, with elementary mathematics.

# 4

## ON THE PATH TO MATHEMATICS

The considerations of the previous chapters have brought us to the point where we can achieve an understanding of how elementary mathematical domains are 'constituted', and how we can gain entrance to them. This would enable us to see how to go about evaluating the sense in which mathematical objects exist. But before proceeding it would be useful to take an overview of the main ideas we have developed so far.

For Husserl, acts of consciousness are 'intentional': they have the character of being directed toward objects. These purported objects may be objects in ontological regions ('objects in worlds') or, analogically, ontological regions ('worlds') themselves. As Husserl repeatedly remarks, all such acts have the form of the *cogito*, the 'I think'. Each such act is a thinking of something, and for each such act we can describe or bring to explicating attention what is thought in or through the act. This is called 'the noematic content' of the act, or simply 'noema'. Each noema bears within it, or has as a part of it, a noematic sense which in some serious measure frames the purported or intended object of thought. It is only by virtue of such a noematic sense that we can have an object as something to be thought about. We cannot work backwards from an object somehow grasped without the utilization of a noematic sense, for all objects are grasped through or on the basis of such a noematic sense. We cannot define the correlations between noematic sense and objects from some absolute point of view because each and every object is grasped through senses, or, more fully, noemata. Like Frege (recall his rejection of correspondence theories of truth discussed in the Introduction;

or see his essay, 'Thoughts'),[1] Husserl would have disparaged some realist or physicalist philosophies of language wherein reference is explained in terms implying that one can somehow grasp the referents themselves antecedently to the senses framing them.

As we observed in Chapter 3, noematic senses typically do not frame objects only on the basis of components which, when reflected on by us, yield descriptions of the purported object as meant, as intended, as thought. Rather, they also prescribe how the purported object can be further thought about, how it can be reasoned about, and how it can be brought to an increasingly determinate and complete grasp. How one might come to notice this is easy enough to understand. If, for example, I wanted to determine the color of the underside of the chair I am sitting on, I would not get out a telescope and look at the Horsehead Nebula, nor would I determine the roots of $5x^2+3x-7=0$; instead, I would lean over, look and see. Something prescribes how I should achieve a more determinate awareness of what I mean to be thinking about, how I should go on to acquire more knowledge of it. More deeply, the noematic sense regulates, or otherwise determines, what bearing any act of consciousness, such as perceptions and observations and thought, has on bringing the purported object of thought to a more complete grasp. It might take quite a bit of thought and work to bring out the bearing it has, but in principle it is determined by the noematic sense. If it were not, then there would be room for deep incoherencies. There would be no grounds for saying that such and such a course of thinking or experience has such and such a bearing on the considered object. Still more deeply, the noema conditions the possible questions we can ask about the object. We may have to use our imagination to dream up such a question, but once it has been dreamt up, it is only perhaps deep and extended reflection on what we intend or mean by the object, that enables us to decide whether or not the question is a fitting one.

1 Gottlob Frege, 'Thoughts', in his *Logical investigations*.

For objects which are as Husserl says 'rationally posited' there will be an explicable relationship of the following sort. Suppose that I am directing my attention toward an object. Then this act will bear within its noematic sense a means of referring to an ontological region or 'world' $O$ in which the object purportedly occurs: some aspect of the noematic sense will have the character of framing $O$. This sense in turn will determine the possible questions which can be asked about this domain and also determine exactly the bearing of all possible mental acts (perceptions, observations, extended acts of reasoning and inferring, and so on) on this domain. I wrote this relationship as

$$\mathrm{Val}_O(A,S),$$

which says that the act of consciousness or mental act $A$ validates $S$[2] or, less correctly, justifies asserting $S$. As was shown in the Introduction and Chapter 1, justifiability does not imply truth; what is at issue is only 'validity' in the sense discussed in the Introduction.

We may regard the relation $\mathrm{Val}_O$ as determining all possible pairs $(A,S)$ such that $A$ is a possible mental act and $S$ is a sentence relevant to $O$. Actually thinking up possible mental acts $A$ and possible questions $S$? may be very difficult and not determined by any algorithmic generating process, but once we have thought up an idea for a mental act $A$ and a question $S$?, then, if $O$ is a rationally posited ontological region, we should be able to decide whether or not $\mathrm{Val}_O(A,S)$. If the relation $\mathrm{Val}_O$ were indecisive here, then $O$ would stand before us as in some respects ill-conceived, as indeed a 'world' would be if we could not tell whether a question were a question about it, or whether or not a group of considerations, $A$, were decisive for it.

We shall have more to say about these $\mathrm{Val}_O$s and how they are implicit in Husserl's texts in the next chapter. But the most important idea behind them is that it is ultimately on their

---

2 Such $\mathrm{Val}_O$s were tacitly present in our studies in Chapter 3, p. 76, e.g. $O$ is 'what is before me in the fog'; it was on the basis of a $\mathrm{Val}_O$ that $O$ was seen to be a dog.

basis that an ontological region or 'world' becomes 'constituted', that is, becomes manifest and accessible to us. The clarification of the science of (in a generous sense) 'the principles of reasoning' about an ontological region is based upon an analysis of the relevant $Val_O$. What I propose to do now is to attempt an analysis of how such a core feature of noematic sense is built up.

We might hope to gain access to such relations of validation Val simply by a direct reflection. But it is seemingly always the case that this is very difficult, exactly because sciences, while practiced under the influence of such a core sense, are practiced, as Husserl says, 'naïvely', producing compounded confusions, so that one suspects that for no science is there an underlying $Val_O$ of sufficient integrity to ensure that the ontological regions which are the concerns of those sciences are 'rationally posited'. One must instead attempt to make new beginnings by patching up or reconstructing 'the principles of reasoning' utilized by the sciences. But to do this we must learn how it is to be done, and to learn this we must attempt to do it in fairly elementary situations, such as elementary mathematics can provide. Husserl gives us no worked out examples; his late *Crisis of the European sciences and transcendental phenomenology* may be regarded as an orienting sketch clearing the way for making a beginning, but principally for the natural sciences, as *FTL* prepared the way for such a foundation for logic. Thus the following is a kind of thought experiment, carried out in an especially simple situation, in which I try to make it a little more than 'just plausible' that we can construct $Val_O$s genuinely constitutive of 'rationally posited' worlds.

I will proceed now with the phenomenological thought experiment. It seems heuristically better simply to proceed without commentary and then afterwards to review what has been done, pulling out and developing an appreciation of its significance. This example and the ensuing discussion will pave the way for the ontological discussion of the next chapter. The main point of the thought experiment is to begin to understand how we can gain access to, constitute, ontological

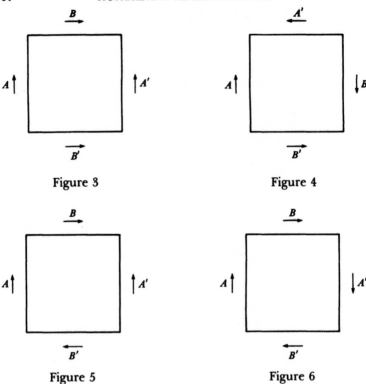

Figure 3                    Figure 4

Figure 5                    Figure 6

regions or domains which are infinite and whose entities seem to be real.

Consider now Figures 3–6, attending to the drawn squares. The objects meant are the drawings, the squares as drawn, figures we might cut out by cutting on the lines. They are of course not perfect Euclidean squares; the lines have width making the boundaries imprecise, the lines have a definite length but only in so far as they are measurable by fairly imprecise measuring instruments. A strong magnifying glass would reveal that we cannot be definite about their length. Likewise the angles are not exact right angles, and so on. I say all of this simply to ensure that the meant objects as meant are the drawn squares; they are not meant as drawings of Euclidean squares, as imperfect representations of somehow perfect geometric figures. If you insist that 'square' can only mean Euclidean square, I would insist that then you should think that I am using 'square' neologistically to mean drawings like these.

Our starting point is therefore with acts of consciousness directed toward and perceptually presentative of objects in the material–visual world about us, viz. the particular objects which you find labelled Figures 3–6. The pages and the drawings are framed or meant as being in the world in which we live, act, and have our being. We can touch the paper; we can tear it; we can cut it; we can cut it on the drawn lines; we can cut out the squares; we can fold and bend them in any number of ways; we can glue edges together; we can cut holes in them. We can make a variety of constructions from them by cutting and pasting. Furthermore we can make further drawings on them. We can talk about the squares, we can draw on them and talk about the drawings, we can perhaps also interpret the drawings in various ways, and so on.

I have been mentioning ideas for activities which can be performed or executed with respect to the paper, ideas which occur to me because of how I construe what I am seeing and also because I have some ideas about what you can and cannot do with paper. I know, for example, that you cannot stretch paper very much. It quickly tears. However, drawing upon my ideas of what is possible in this world in which I find myself living and acting, I could imagine that the drawings were on a more flexible and stretchable material. I can imagine myself stretching the material in many directions and having it keep the form into which I stretch it. By imagining myself stretching it I could, by suppressing ideas about what materials are not available, imagine myself stretching it indefinitely. So it is that I look at the drawn squares and imagine them being cut out – I can imagine myself doing this, cutting them out – and then imagine their edges being pasted together in certain ways. The latter is dependent on my having the idea that indeed I could paste the edges of the cut-out squares together in certain ways, although not in all the ways that I can imagine pasting them together if I imagined the squares having been drawn on a very plastic material.

Thus it is that I begin to imagine objects which although closely related to objects in this world are not part of it. Nevertheless because I am drawing so heavily on ideas of objects which I can see and touch in this world, and objects which I can act on in certain ways and perform certain constructions with, I do not have any sense of pushing my ideas and conceptions beyond any limits, but just of suppressing some facts.

But now I do take a bit of a leap, drawing on my numerical imagination. I imagine that there are available as many cut-out squares as I like – $10^{10}$ or $100^{100}$ or however many. Here I am drawing upon and utilizing an idea, that of the natural number series, to extend my imagination beyond what I can concretely exhibit to myself in imagination, while suspending beliefs about what can be done in the world about me. It may be that a very refined analysis of all the ideas and conceptions I am drawing upon, attending to delicate distinctions and all the rules which give cogency to discourse, would reveal that there is no room for the kind of imaginings I am undertaking, but there is no evidence that this is so. A perfectly adequate phenomenology would require that we go into all such details, but let us just assume that everything is all right at present, and see if a line of thinking emerges which would make such a refined analysis worthwhile, a line of thinking revealing a path into mathematical worlds, into ontological regions distinct from that in which I find myself living and acting.

Thus we have before us in imagination an infinity of cut-out squares made of a stretchable material, capable of forming different shapes and which can be pasted together in various ways. Looking ahead a bit, I find that as far as imagining 'pasting together' is concerned, I do not have to imagine an activity of pasting. The effect I will want is just that two edges are brought into coincidence, are in some way identified. But how this is to be understood, how it is to be thought about, remains to be considered.

Let us reconsider the figures, attending to the letters and the arrows. I now interpret the latter as rules for pasting cut-out edges together. The idea is that edge $A$ is pasted onto edge $A'$ so that the directions of the arrows match; likewise for $B$ and $B'$. (In constructing these basic objects, we may only bend, stretch and paste. We may not tear, although in order to construct more complex objects out of these basic objects we may cut holes in their surfaces and paste them together at the rims of the holes, as described below.)

Consider first Figures 3 and 4. Let us carry out in imagination the construction prescribed by Figure 3. Smoothly bending $A$ over to meet $A'$, then 'pasting' the edges together, we get something which is or can be formed into a tube, a hollow open-ended cylinder. Now imagine bringing $B$ around to meet $B'$, so that one open end of the tube meets the other. We can see that open end to open end, the arrows match, so we can 'paste' the two ends together, the result being something like a hollow ring, a so-called *torus*.

Now let us do the same for Figure 4. We 'paste' $A$ and $A'$ together, the result being something which could be shaped into a cone with an open base. We see that $B$ and $B'$ are in a position where the directions of the arrows match, so we can 'paste' $B$ and $B'$ together. The result is a kind of close envelope which we can imagine as being expanded and shaped into a *sphere*.

We can imagine thus making as many tori and spheres as we please, cutting holes in their surfaces and pasting them together, hole matching hole, in infinite varieties of ways. Perhaps we attach a large number of tori or a large number of tori and spheres to one sphere in this way, and to each of those we attach large varieties of tori or tori and spheres, and so on. So, relying on our numerical imagination, we can construct infinite varieties of such objects.

We have here the appearance of having before us an infinite domain of entities which, although formed on the basis of ideas and ideas of activities having to do with the world that we find ourselves in, are something apart, for we have suppressed all of the facts which would have confined our projected constructions to those which could be carried out in this world. Perhaps indeed this world we find ourselves in is infinite and materials of the right sort exist, perhaps indeed in this world infinite processes can be completed in a finite amount of time; but this is irrelevant to what we have imagined, drawing as it does on support from our numerical imagination, or, better, our conception of the natural number series.

Let us now consider Figures 5 and 6. We can paste together sides $A$ and $A'$ in Figure 5, arrows matching, again forming a tube. Now we must join together $B$ and $B'$, the two open ends of the tube, so that the arrows match, but now we find that when we bend the ends around so that they meet, the arrows do not match. Thus we cannot join them together as we did in the case of Figure 3. How else can we join them together? The only other possibility (short of tearing a hole in the surface, which we do not allow) is to invaginate one end and draw it through to meet the other end from the inside, hoping that in this way the directions of the arrows will match. But by carefully picturing the situation to ourselves, we find that they do not. We cannot carry out the construction. The situation Figure 6 confronts us with is even more difficult. The first step requires that we twist the 'paper' in order to bring $A$ and $A'$ into coincidence so that the arrows match. Then after an even more extended exercise than was necessary in the case of Figure 5, we see that we cannot bring $B$ and $B'$ together in the necessary way. This construction cannot be carried out either.

But now we ask ourselves, since 'pasting' in imagination simply comes to identifying the edges so that the arrows match, why can we not just identify the edges $B$ and $B'$ in Figures 5 and 6? That is, why can we not just use a sort of 'logical glue' and say by fiat, 'identify $B$ and $B'$, arrows matching in direction', thereby forming a conception of the respective objects? In order to do so we have to give up all possibility of identifying our conception of an object with a conception of something we could find in our environment, such as something shaped like a hollow ring or something shaped like a sphere. There seems to be nothing against this, does there? Well, we have to take a different view of the objects. We cannot conceive of them as being a reconstruction in imagination of the space we visually and actively find ourselves in. Either we have to extend our conception of that space in some difficult way (e.g. extending its dimensions), or we have to construe the objects as being spaces not embedded in another more encompassing space. Then all of those constructions we mediately imagined being possible with tori and spheres can be thought of as constructing different spaces.

The figures constructed by means of 'logical glue' in Figures 5 and 6 are called respectively *Klein bottles* and *projective planes*. Let us imagine throwing them in with the tori and spheres and using them in the same process of construction, namely by cutting holes in their surfaces and 'pasting' them together in all possible ways, effecting entry into a very rich and strange 'world'.

But how do we effect such an entry? We have been playing fast and loose with our imagination, making several unclarified prescriptions, such as the use of 'logical glue' and regarding the objects constructed as spaces not embedded in a larger space, but as, so to speak, spaces in themselves. If they are spaces in themselves how can we talk of their being 'constructed'? We can ask many such questions. We seem indeed to be developing an intrinsically incoherent discourse, to be forcing our ideas to adapt to leaps of imagination which increasingly threaten incoherence and inconsistency. Whereas, in our first acts of imagination in connection with Figures 3 and 4, it did not seem that we were stretching the ideas we were using in any especially dangerous way (we were simply abstracting from what is factually possible), it now seems that we are pushing our way toward conceptions which are logically questionable, e.g. figures we imagine to be constructed in space but whose construction requires or seems to require that we imagine them as being spaces in themselves, and so on.

If we reflect on our considerations so far we find that they are defective in a way not unlike those carried out for arithmetic in Husserl's *Philosophie der Arithmetik*: we have nowhere instituted principles of reasoning for the objects or purported objects we have attempted to bring ourselves to recognize. At best we can say of them that they are objects which can be constructed in certain ways, but even this is very obscure in that we have had to appeal to notions which do not obviously cohere with the ideas we draw from the resources we use to think about and understand the world about us (if indeed this 'world' about us is framed and posited with sufficient cogency for us to speak of 'it' as '*the* world'). Because of the ideas of 'logical glue' and of objects being spaces in themselves, the purported objects cannot be clearly given to us in our visual imagination (perhaps we could imagine ourselves as somehow 'in' their 'surface', but this is already stretching things quite a bit, not to mention the difficulty of *imagining* a 'surface' not itself contained in a space).

If we had to rely on the ideas we have developed so far, I think it must be said that the purported objects we have attempted to describe are not rational posits, possible objects of thinking and reasoning. Perhaps, one might think, if we went through our considerations once more with greater care, then we could manage to have them as rational posits. But all we could be clearer about are the incoherencies, the employment of ideas (such as 'spaces in themselves') for which no adequate ground can be prepared in our spatial imagination, no ground adequate to assure that principles for thinking and reasoning about the purported objects would be forthcoming.

Rather, these principles must be decided upon. We can regard ourselves as having developed vague ideas of mathematical objects; but what we need is to choose principles which would produce a clear and cogent 'conception', in short a $\text{Val}_O$ of some integrity. At the same time these cannot be arbitrarily chosen principles, for we want to preserve something of our emerging though not altogether clear and coherent idea of these purported '2-manifolds'.

How do we proceed? At the very least we need (perhaps equally vague) ideas of coherent properties and relations. Only one stands out so far: that two constructed 2-manifolds are the same if they can be regarded as being constructed in the same way. Suppose that I think of a 2-manifold as being constructed from a Klein bottle by cutting holes and pasting on a torus and a sphere, and then pasting on the sphere five projective planes and then on the torus 2-manifolds obtained by pasting together in all possible ways five tori, seven spheres, fourteen projective planes, and ten Klein bottles. Then every 2-manifold which can be regarded as having been constructed in the same way (even though it was not, for I could take any component 2-manifold in the above construction and make it my starting point) is equal to it.

It might seem that despite the extreme difficulty in imagining and comparing such objects, the relation of identity is well defined. After all, we do not have to rely on imagination at all; we could just use letters as signs for the different ingredients connecting them with lines showing what is pasted to what, as is indeed suggested by the very description I gave. Then we just have to study two such sign systems and see if they can be brought into a correspondence in which components correspond to components and pastings to pastings.

The difficulty is that, since we are allowing 'stretchability' in the 'material' of which the 2-manifolds are 'made', it might happen that 2-manifolds built up out of many 2-manifolds reduce to one of the four simple 2-manifolds. For example, two spheres glued together (by, as above, cutting out holes in each and gluing them together on the edges of the holes) when appropriately stretched (without tearing) and reshaped are clearly (by an exercise of visual imagination) equivalent to one sphere; while if we have five spheres and the first is glued to the second (remember the gluing process proceeds by cutting out holes and then gluing the objects together at the rims of the holes), the second to the third, the third to the fourth, the fourth to the fifth, and the fifth to the first, we get a torus.

Well, we seem to have recognized a difficulty and discovered that our imagination was adequate to overcoming it, discovering simultaneously that there already seem to be some principles of 'reasoning' at work guiding our imagination. We could even begin to formulate such principles. They are founded on the imagining of stretching and reshaping without tearing. Thus we can give more cogency to our principle of identity: two 2-manifolds are identical if they can be regarded as being built up in the same way, perhaps by reorganizing our conception of them on the basis of permitted stretchings and reshapings. We could even begin to develop a little calculus, e.g. whenever two spheres composing a considered 2-manifold are pasted together we can regard them as one sphere, or one sphere can be regarded as two spheres pasted together under some arbitrary distribution between them of the 2-manifolds glued on to the original sphere.

This principle of reasoning was not however forced. We could have simply arbitrarily asserted that when two 2-manifolds are pasted together (always, remember, cutting out holes and pasting together the rims of the holes) using only small holes, they become rigid, or at most a small portion of them can be pulled out (as a kind of pseudopod) in order to make it possible to attach other 2-manifolds. Then it would not be possible for, say, two spheres glued together to be transformed in imagination into one sphere by reshaping. (Of course we would also have to give a conventional shape to the objects constructed from diagrams of Figures 3 and 4.) These would be rather boring objects, but, in any case, this point of view could hardly be maintained once we throw in the objects constructed on the basis of Figures 5 and 6, the Klein bottles and projective planes, for we cannot give them standard shapes in imagination.

In the latter case it is also much harder to see that, for example, a torus and projective plane connected together is the same thing as pasting together three projective planes. That can be seen by going back and using drawings of the sort utilized in Figures 3–6, but now drawing holes on them, indicating where they are pasted together, and making various sorts of artful

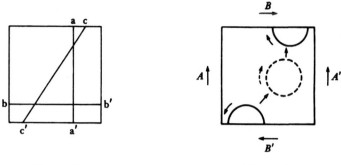

Figure 7                              Figure 8

and simplifying observations.[3] But lest we get involved with too many complicated considerations which simply distract us from what is essential, let us consider another axis along which we can obtain ideas for properties.

Return to the original figures, but consider now Figure 7. If it is regarded as Figure 3 with lines drawn on it, then the line cc′ cannot exist on it, for only points on the edges which are directly opposite to one another are identified. If it is regarded as Figure 6, then for similar reasons aa′ and bb′ cannot exist on it. If it is regarded as Figure 5, then only bb′ and cc′ can exist on it, and if it is regarded as Figure 4, then none of the lines indicated can exist on it. Thus we have obtained an idea for properties which distinguish the elementary 2-manifolds from one another, and we might ask if analogous properties extended to all possible 2-manifolds somehow correspond to those preserved under the criterion of identity that we gave, viz. the 'lines' which can exist on them can exactly distinguish them.

This seems complicated and points the way toward an idea for another property, e.g. two closed lines ('bands') on a 2-manifold are 'equivalent' if we can imagine moving and stretching (without tearing) one line until it is brought into coincidence with the other. On the torus there are three such 'equivalence classes' of lines (including a circle drawn in the

3 cf. W. S. Massey, *Algebraic topology: an introduction* (Berlin, 1967), Chapter I.

center of Figure 7 forming the basis of the third equivalence class); on the sphere, only one. On the projective plane? On the Klein bottle?

Analogous reflections yield ideas for further possible properties. For example, imagine a circle drawn with an arrow giving it a direction or orientation such as in Figure 8, and suppose the indicated construction of a Klein bottle to be carried out. What happens as we move this circle around?

Before we can answer this, we have to reach a decision, which we should long ago have acknowledged. The problem is, does a figure such as a line or a circle lie 'in' the surface or 'on' the surface, i.e. does it lie on one side or on both sides simultaneously? The piece of paper makes it possible for a figure to be on one side but not the other. Do we want this property to be preserved in our manifolds? It is exactly here that the idea of the 2-manifolds being spaces in themselves arises. There is simply no space for them to be on the surface rather than in the surface. Furthermore, we do not necessarily want the surface to have thickness. That would create further deep problems. If we could think of the surfaces as having no thickness, then our objects would be wonderfully simpler. But can we manage this? It seems that we can prescribe it by saying that a line is in the surface in the sense that, as in Figure 8, the circle can be moved round as indicated and brought to occupy the same space, so that there is no 'room' for a circle to exist 'above' or 'below' it. But this is merely a suggestion. Here is another idea for a property the analysis of which would perhaps require an analysis or explanation of our manifolds in terms of a point–line structure.

Now when we turn the circle around as in Figure 8, we find that the arrow now points in the opposite direction. This will happen for the Klein bottle and projective plane, but not for the sphere or the torus. This suggests a new property for 2-manifolds, viz. 'orientability', which we can now explore in connection with the other properties. Indeed, several problems come to mind: whether our criterion for identity is adequate in the sense that any two 2-manifolds which are

identical (according to it) will be such that the number of
equivalence classes of closed lines will be the same, whether
they are both orientable or non-orientable. (In both cases I am
thinking of the two 2-manifolds before the series of analyses
and transformations which show they can be regarded as
being built up in the same way.) We confront deeper problems
about how to show that the equivalence classes of lines which
we can compute from the drawings are exactly all that is possible. In the synthetic but not quite *a priori* 'proofs' we have
been contemplating so far, we have to hunt for the different
possibilities. We cannot be certain that we have left none out.
Obviously greater explicitness about the 'principles' we tacitly
use (such as imagined indefinite stretchability) will not
necessarily help us to close things off, to be certain that our
imagination has not been faulty, that it has not overlooked
cases.

Indeed the ideas for properties and relations which have
emerged, involving as they do elements of ideas which are
intended for application in the world we find about us, are
ideas which are liable at any moment to introduce confusion
and incoherence. Furthermore our considerations are also
pointing us toward a conception of 2-manifolds which needs
to be distinguished from an (infinite) plane or a 2-manifold
obtained by deforming a plane in any way that does not tear it.
Since we identify our 2-manifolds if they can be regarded as
having been constructed in the same way, we cannot provide
them with a 'metric', with a concept of 'distance', for we
regard, for example, two spheres as identical no matter how
large they are (as far as our imaginative construction of
them is concerned).

There are two things to be noticed about what we have done
so far.

Despite obscurities about our ideas, and about the ideas of
our objects and their properties, our considerations are pointing
toward a coherent and consistent conception, though because
of all the residual elements in these ideas (mentioned above)
we are far from having achieved it. This shows up in our being

able to arrive at certain 'truths', e.g. spheres have only one equivalence class of lines, two spheres glued together (at the rims of holes cut in each) are 'identical' with one sphere, and so on.

We cannot say that the domain of 2-manifolds of the sort we are interested in is rationally posited, but we can see a way in which it might be. We begin just by making a list of all of the statements we find ourselves wanting to make about the 2-manifolds and then looking for principles for reasoning by means of them. Since we will form these statements from terms used in talking about the world we find ourselves in, aspects of their use lead to incoherencies such as:

(1) a 2-manifold is a space in itself,
(2) we consider the 2-manifolds constructed in imagination from Figures 3–6 by 'pasting' the edges together as required, and then . . .

It is hard to carry out (2) without an appeal to a performance within imagined space, which then conflicts with (1), not to mention our inability to do this for Klein bottles and projective planes. Nevertheless, we seem to be able to suppress or side-step these various incoherencies by not utilizing, by not paying attention to those elements in our ideas which lead to incoherencies.

By proceeding in a naïve way and not attending to all that we have been utilizing in our thinking, it may seem that we have 'abstracted' the fundamental ideas, and that they are in our grasp in their mathematical purity, free from all of the incoherencies our use of them and their sources carry in discourse and thought about the ordinary world. But – and this is the important point – it is not so. We still have a great deal of work to do. We must set out *principles of reasoning about the 2-manifolds* (which seem to have been more and more definitely conceived as we proceeded) *which in no way depend upon those elements in our ideas which are the source of incoherencies*. (They are such a source because they are intended for application in a quite different ontological region: the world we find ourselves in.)

In some of our considerations above we had an illusion of having established synthetic *a priori* truths. But this is an illusion exactly because the sentences we used to express these 'truths' involved as part of their sense notions fitted only to the world about us. Only by instituting new principles of reasoning can those sentences and their component expressions be used in thinking, side-stepping the incoherencies which their normal context and use produce (as described above). Then, and only then, can the '2-manifolds' we have been considering become rational posits.

I will not proceed further with this particular example, for the next stages of thinking about it are too complicated to be worth pursuing to make the observations I want to make. I have chosen the example because one could very quickly get to a *mélange* of 'intuitions' pointing toward a mathematical domain, while at the same time seeing clearly the problems which stand in the way. In order to illustrate *how* the next step is taken – the instituting of principles of reasoning which simultaneously institute a new discourse using terms from discourse about the world about us, and use them to frame and reason about otherworldly mathematical objects – I will retreat to elementary geometry, contriving an analogous circumstance.

In paragraph 20 of Investigation II of *LI* Husserl says:

Is Berkeley not right in insisting that, when we prove a proposition relating to all triangles, we have, on any occasion, only one triangle in mind, the one in our drawing, and that we make use of the features that characterize a triangle as a triangle, while ignoring all others? . . . Berkeley speaks as if geometric proofs were conducted for the triangle drawn in ink on the paper or in chalk on the blackboard, as if the chance singulars which float before us in general thought, were not mere aids to our thoughts intentions, but its actual objects. A geometrical procedure which took its lead from the *drawn* figure in Berkeley's sense, might yield astonishing results, but scarcely very happy ones. No geometric proposition holds for the drawn figure as a physical object, since the latter is not really rectilinear, nor a geometrical figure at all.

In his 'Die natürliche Geometrie' of 1923, the Danish geometer Hjelmslev attempted to construct a geometry of drawn figures.[4] In such a geometry there are many peculiarities distinguishing it from Euclid's geometry. For example, two circles of differing radius can coincide for an arc (rather than just a point, as in the ideal case their difference in curvature demands); the base angles of isosceles triangles (triangles with at least two sides equal) need not be equal; a circle and a line tangent to it can coincide for an arc (and not just a point). These things are the case because in the first and last case, this is how the drawings look, and one cannot draw them so perfectly that they look otherwise. In the case of an isosceles triangle having unequal base angles, this is at least implied by the fact that two circles of unequal radius can coincide for an arc.

As I have already pointed out in the Introduction, such a geometry requires at least deviant principles of equality, for, because of the possibilities of accumulating differences below the threshold of detectability, for some series of triangles, the principle of the transitivity of equality, when applied reiteratively, may fail.

Consider now Figures 9 and 10. Figure 9 is a drawing of an isosceles triangle. Are the base angles equal? One standard 'argument' is, yes, because of bilateral symmetry. But now consider Figure 10 where two drawn circles of unequal radius unavoidably coincide for an arc. Because lines $A'$ and $A''$ are radii of circle $A$, and because lines $B'$ and $B''$ are radii of circle $B$ the triangles $CA'A''$ and $C'B'B''$ are both isosceles triangles, but it is obvious from the drawing that the base angles are not equal, for one base angle of the first triangle is *inside of* a base angle of the second triangle, while the other base angle of the first triangle is *outside of* the base angle of the other triangle.

We then have two proofs 'by intuition', one proved assertion contradicting the other. Indeed, if we insist that the base angles of an isosceles triangle cannot be equal, then two

---

4 J. Hjelmslev, 'Die natürliche Geometrie', *Hamburger Mathematische Einzelschriften*, part 1 (1923), pp. 1–36.

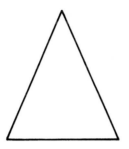

Figure 9

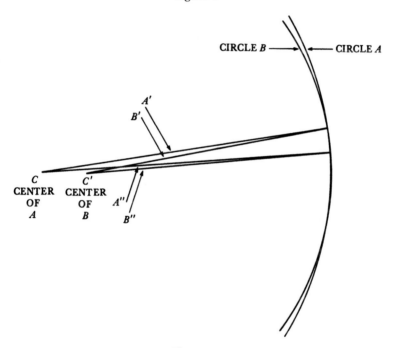

Figure 10

circles of unequal radius (or two circles of equal radius with
different centers) can coincide for an arc.

Of course we can hardly claim to have proved 'theorems' in
either case. *At most we have ideas for proofs and theorems.* In particular we have not provided what is absolutely essential for

assuring that our assertions express something about cogent
and well-conceived objects, for we have provided no principles
of reasoning.

We can observe, however, that if we want the base angle
theorem to hold, the 'objects', the triangles about which this
theorem holds, cannot belong to the ontological region of
Hjelmslev's geometry, for it contradicts one of the most
obvious 'truths' of that geometry, viz. that two circles of unequal radius can coincide for an arc.

Consider now the expressions:

(1) The base angles of isosceles triangles are equal.
(2) Two circles of unequal radius cannot coincide for an arc.

Let us first understand the thoughts behind these sentences as
being composed of senses adapted to the ontological region of
Hjelmslev's geometry, viz. the region of *drawn* figures. In this
region (1) is false and (2) is false, while in Euclid's geometry
they are both true.

But now suppose we assert that (1) is true. Then, by our pictorial argument in Figure 9, (2) will be true. The pictorial argument is an argument of some cogency and interest, for the
truth of (2) obviously leads to a theorem to the effect that all
triangles are rigid. But the pictorial argument was exactly that:
the principles behind the argument were not laid down.

We can take the sentences (1) and (2) which we regard as
expressing the sense appropriate for the Hjelmslevian
domain, preserving the sentences, but now instituting principles
of reasoning, principles about the purported objects, which
allow for the inference of (2) from (1), but which do not allow
us to secure the falsity of (2) by appealing to drawings. For
example, we could set down the principle of the transitivity of
equality and the principle that two triangles are equal if two
corresponding sides and their corresponding angle are equal,
and so on, enabling us to derive the theorem that the base
angles of isosceles triangles are equal. The principle of
Hjelmslev's geometry, that between any two points we can
construct a straight line joining them, can be maintained as

well as the definition that a circle is constructed by a compass
and the definition that a triangle is a figure constructed by
joining three points not on the same line by lines. By proceeding
in this manner we can carry out a demonstration according to
such principles showing that the base angles of isosceles
triangles are equal and that no two circles of unequal radius
can coincide for an arc. But all of the meanings of the terms I
am using have changed. They no longer refer to *drawn* figures.
And yet, at the same time, the principles of reasoning
instituted were inspired by brooding over drawings. We point
to a picture of two 'circles' in the Hjelmslevian sense which
appear to be coinciding for an arc, but now say that these
objects must be reasoned about in this way (giving principles
of the sort we have described above, principles of the sort laid
down in Book I of Euclid's *Elements*). Without the Hjelmslevian
domain and the correlated domain of sense we would not
have found our way into the Euclidean domain; we found our
way by looking at the Hjelmslevian discourse and imposing
on it different principles of reasoning. The underlying
Hjelmslevian senses are still present, enabling us to find our
way to drawings, but those drawings are now 'read' according
to the newly instituted principles of reasoning. We can thus
interpret the drawings as approximating to the Euclidean
figures, as representing them, but this does not adequately
describe their function.

To understand their function, return for a moment to the
domain of 2-manifolds we were beginning to enter earlier.
Suppose that I had proceeded by instituting principles of
reasoning in a way analogous to the way I have just indicated
for Euclidean figures. But now suppose that I did not yet have
the idea of the property of 'orientability'. Although the objects
framed by the emerging theory are incompletely imagined
constructs, out of paper or whatever, the expressions I am
using according to newly instituted principles of reasoning
still carry with them, or can have conferred on them, the old
senses, relating them back to the domain of imagined constructions, a domain ill-framed and incoherently thought

through those senses. But in any case they provide the path back to a point where I could continue my imaginative play, hunting for *ideas* of properties, such as orientability, which I could then hope to transfer upwards, making them exact by instituting principles of reasoning about them coherent with those principles already instituted. That is, I could always return to the original domain and attempt there to acquire new ideas for properties or relations, and, indeed, theorems and proofs, which I could hope to transfer to the new domain by instituting principles of reasoning compatible with the new ideas and compatible with the already instituted principles of reasoning.

Let us draw back and take an overview. What is the emerging pattern?

How do we gain access to, 'constitute', make manifest, at least elementary mathematical domains? The way I have been pursuing this question was suggested by Husserl's late essay 'The origins of geometry'.[5] The problem as Husserl sees it is to reactivate the originating *Evidenzen* which make geometry possible and give its propositions 'validity'. In the English editions, *Evidenz* is translated 'self-evidence', which is rather misleading since 'self-evidence' implies that there is nothing more to say. When I have been talking about 'principles of reasoning' I have had in mind, indeed, 'principles of *Evidenzen*', principles conferring or withholding 'validity' (the reader will recall the discussion of this notion in the Introduction). *Evidenz* is, so to speak, the appearance of validity (which may or may not entail 'objective truth' or 'absolute truth'). In so far as the 'principles of *Evidenzen*' are explicable, to that extent it is incorrect to speak of 'self-evidence'. The one justification for speaking in this way is that there is no absolute test to ensure that the principles are applied correctly; one perhaps just has to *see that* they are. For example, I can give rules for adding up numbers written in standard arabic decimal notation. To check my work I must check whether I have applied the rules

5 Edmund Husserl, 'The origins of geometry', Appendix VI of his *Crisis of the European sciences and transcendental phenomenology*.

correctly. The best I can do is rehearse the rules and examine my use of them. I cannot supply rules for checking that I have applied the rules correctly; or, if I could, I would encounter exactly the same problem for these rules, and so on *ad infinitum*. We have ultimately to rely on our understanding of what we intend to be doing when applying the rules and what it 'looks like' to have applied them correctly. It is this which is the essence of Husserl's notion of *Evidenz*; roughly speaking, *Evidenz* is the awareness of accomplishing what one has set out to do, or it is how that accomplishment shows itself.

More precisely, in para. 59 of *FTL* Husserl writes:

*Evidenz* . . . designates that performance on the part of intentionality which consists in the giving of something itself.

'Giving of something itself' is understood in a delicate way. This 'giving of' is nothing more or less than what makes it possible to see that one has done what one has intended to do, e.g. that one is seeing what one means to be seeing. And *this* is to be understood from the point of view of 'validity': the noemata prescribe what sort of acts of consciousness can be 'validated' as a seeing of such and such.

Thus to reactivate the originating *Evidenzen* for elementary mathematics, such as Euclid's Book I, is just to make explicit the originating noematic senses, essentially involving as they do the 'principles of reason' or 'principles of validation'.

How do we build up such a sense, indeed, such a Val? What are our materials? For Husserl the starting point is essentially 'the lived-world', the *Lebenswelt*, which together with its discourses forms what he called a 'meaning fundament' (paras. 10ff. of the *Crisis*). The *Lebenswelt* is the world in which we live and act and have our being. It is the world whose principal *logos* or discourse is provided by ordinary language. Thus the problem of the origins of geometry is that of describing how we get from this world or, rather from the discourse and activities which frame and manifest it, to the discourse or, more exactly, principles of reason, principles of validity, Val, of geometry, or any elementary mathematics (mathematics whose objects are related in some suggestive way to objects given to us in the *Lebenswelt*).

It is wrong, of course, to speak of *the* 'lived-world', since its character changes in time and from culture to culture. In his 'The origins of geometry' (and his *Crisis*) Husserl attempted to make it evident that all 'lived-worlds' share an invariant structure in terms of which we could carry out an 'absolute' description of the origins of geometry. Some philosophers, such as Derrida, are convinced that Husserl did not and could not establish that. Roughly, as in the later Wittgenstein, this is because there are no invariant laws, no pure reason as it were, to which all 'discourses' must conform. However, it might be the case that all discourses framing 'lived-worlds', on whose basis one could find one's way to mathematics, might all necessarily share such an invariant structure.

In any case, whatever might be decided about this matter in the future, the examples I have sketched suggest that we can indeed provide an account of the 'origins' of elementary mathematics on the foundation of our *Lebenswelt*.

I began by attending to a particular sphere of noematic sense framing certain aspects of the lived-world (and so I began with certain 'parts' of Val$_{lived-world}$), e.g. those framing drawings on pieces of paper, drawings framed as being susceptible to our being able to act on them in certain ways. Inspired by what is thus given to us, we utilized this noematic background (including a kind of 'background theory' loosely specifying what we take to be facts of the matter for the world in which we find ourselves) in the development of a kind of imaginative play. Our play (e.g. imagining certain constructions performed with imagined materials), which was expressible throughout by a discourse whose sense derives from the noematic background (the background of 'thought' framing the relevant aspects of the lived-world), was put under various strains and stresses, introducing incoherencies, which, however, we could in some measure side-step sufficiently to begin to develop ideas of objects, properties, arguments, and truths which seemed to stand before our minds despite the incoherencies. But this seeming was indeed illusory, for we had not clearly and firmly instituted a new discourse, a new *logos*, principles of reasoning, principles of validity, a Val, which was, on the one hand, compatible with the emerging ideas of objects, properties, arguments, and truths, but, on the other hand, not beset by their incoherencies and vagaries.

Perhaps, to make things plainer, it would be useful to spell out the second example a bit more.

In the setting of the world we find about us, we can talk about straight lines and drawn straight lines, drawn circles, and so on. The former are such as can be drawn with a straight edge, the latter are such as can be drawn with a compass. By the nature of the construction with a compass we can think of any point we choose on the circle as being the same distance from the center (where the compass point touched). 'Same distance' can mean 'measurably the same' or even 'looks the same'; if actual measuring showed discrepancies, these could be traced to our misuse of the compass. We can think of triangles as figures formed from three drawn lines *AB, CD, EF*, the ends *A* and *C* coinciding, the ends *D* and *E* coinciding, the ends *B* and *F* coinciding, but no other parts of the three lines coinciding. Then we can understand by 'isosceles triangles' triangles as figures formed from three drawn lines *AB, CD, EF*, length. All 'exactness' here is the 'exact inexactness' which is part of our discourse in the lived-world.

We can think of two triangles or circles as 'being equal' if we assure ourselves that they could be brought to coincide or that their respective parts are measurably the same. One obvious fact about such 'equality' is that it is not preserved under reiterated applications of the principle that two things equal to the same thing are equal to each other, for while

$T_1$ may be equal to $T_2$, $T_2$ to $T_3$, $T_3$ to $T_4$,

$T_1$ may not be equal to $T_4$ because the difference may be detectable by our measuring devices, even though the difference between $T_3$ and $T_4$ is not detectable.

We developed certain arguments, again in the discourse

used for framing such objects within the lived-world, e.g. the argument by pictures that if two circles of unequal radius coincide for an arc, then the base angles of isosceles triangles are not always equal.

By deliberating in this way (as was also illustrated in the example of the '2-manifolds' we considered), a discourse generated within the discourse available to us in our thinking and talking about the lived-world develops, as well as various arguments which are indeed 'valid' within the emerging discourse.

Now by considerations of symmetry or whatever I might be inspired to the following idea: the base angles of isosceles triangles are not always equal because of 'inexactness'. Or we could 'argue' that the equality of the base angles of an isosceles triangle follows from the assumption that two triangles are equal if two of their corresponding sides and the angle determined by them are respectively equal (as in Proposition 5 in Euclid's Book I), but that we cannot accept *this* principle because of 'inexactness'. Suppose that we allow the reiterative use of the principle that two things equal to the same thing are equal to each other and the reiterative use of the principle that two triangles are equal if two sides and the contained angle are respectively equal. Obviously we get into contradictions.

But we can develop a strategy for avoiding such contradictions. We accept the newly instituted principles and all inferences from the discourse (such as, given the principles, two circles of unequal radius cannot coincide for an arc, the base angles of isosceles triangles are equal, triangles are 'rigid', and so on). We are using expressions and some arguments from within the old discourse, but are forcing ourselves to reason with and about them in a different way. We can in an analogous manner proceed to enlarge this new discourse and refine it, instituting further principles which are suggested by considerations analogous to the ones suggested. In this way, it seems that we can eventually produce Book I of Euclid.

In order to understand what is happening, consider for a moment a generalized version of Frege's 'context' principle:

never ask for the meaning of a term independently of sentences in which it rightly occurs. In its generalized form this principle is: never ask for the meaning of a term independently of the discourse in which it occurs. The *logos* of this discourse, the principles of reasoning or *Evidenz* governing it, the underlying Val, fix the objects of reference.

What we have done is to begin with a discourse about drawn figures and *its* underlying Val, but have taken the expressions and imposed a different *logos* on them, a different Val, different principles of validation, of acceptance. 'Triangle' can no longer mean 'triangle as drawn', and so on.

Nevertheless this new discourse is, as Husserl would say, *founded* on the old, *non-independent* of the old, in that it was produced from the old by the imposition of new principles of reasoning, of validity. It is doubtful that the new discourse would have any significance for us if it were not related to the old in that way.

As far as understanding the 'new objects', we could say that the new 'triangles' are related to the old 'triangles' as the perfectly exact to the inexact, but that the actual relationship is precisely spelled out by spelling out the relationship between the old and the new Vals (or the discourses they sustain).

Such an analysis of 'the origins' of elementary mathematics shows us the way to begin to understand much that has been a mystery. For example, once we understand the origins and see that indeed at many points it is possible to make different choices of principles of validation, there is no necessity for, say, the geometry of Book I of Euclid to apply to 'the space around us'. But because the nature of the origin of the geometry was obscure there was the illusion that it applied automatically. The 'validity' of Euclid's Book I lies solely in its 'principles of validation', but because these principles were (seemingly tacitly) instituted by utilizing a discourse valid for the lived-world and because the way of utilizing it was not clear, there was a confusion about the 'meaning' of Euclid's Book I.

Book I could be related to the world as lived because we can always reassociate the old sense from the old discourse with the terms and expressions now occurring in the new discourse. This indeed provides the possibility of applying Book I to 'idealize' aspects of the world we find ourselves in. But this application only proceeded easily because, e.g. Galileo did not realize that he was associating two senses (those from the old discourse and those from the new), but took them to be one.

The connection between the two discourses explains the relevance of pictures to, e.g., the emerging theory of 2-manifolds and the emerging Euclidean geometry. Since such pictures and other visual imaginings provided us with *ideas* for properties, arguments, etc., they could always be utilized. For example, suppose (to make again a point made before) that I had gone on to develop a theory of '2-manifolds' of the sort discussed, but had never arrived at the idea of 'orientability'. Perhaps this property subsequently occurs to me; then I could try to bring 'it' into the new discourse, amplifying the Val of the discourse, instituting principles of reasoning about this property in a coherent and compatible way.

Returning to the example from elementary geometry, I had previously made the analogy (in Chapter 3, p. 62):

$$\frac{\text{Frazer spirals}}{\text{concentric circles}} = \frac{\text{drawn triangles}}{\text{Euclidean triangles}} = \frac{\text{something visible}}{\text{something invisible}}$$

When we look at the Frazer spirals we experience spirals, but these can be construed as a distorted presentation of the drawn circles. But now, in the case of our sketch of a path to Euclid's Book I from a discourse and its attendant noematic background framing aspects of the lived-world to a Val, we can frame the domain of Euclidean figures; we see that the way we followed this path gives each expression in our emerging language for Euclid's geometry a dual role: it can be understood under the Val determining the Hjelmslevian geometry or under the Val determining the Euclidean geometry. The path of modifications and transformations we have laid out, taking us from one understanding to the other, provides us with a way of construing the Hjelmslevian figures as poor but useful representations of the Euclidean figures. However, the exact nature of this 'representation' is determined by the path from the Hjelmslevian Val to the Euclidean Val.

In conclusion, I would like to offer an especially simple example illustrating some of the main ideas developed above.

We can easily form the idea of a series of sequences of stroke-objects,

/  //  ///  ////  /////  //////  ///////  ////////  /////////  . . .,

where the next sequence is obtained by reconstructing the previous sequence and then adding on a /.

We might hope to be able to build up a foundation of arithmetic on the basis of this idea, perhaps construing 'numbers' as the corresponding sign-types (the signs written above being tokens of the types), addition corresponding to concatenation, multiplication of $x$ by $y$ corresponding to substituting a $y$ for each / in $x$, and so on. One might then propose as a possible theorem, e.g. for all $x$ and for all $y$, $x$ multiplied by $y$ yields the same as $y$ multiplied by $x$. It is not immediately obvious that this is so, for it is not obvious that substituting an $x$ for every / in $y$ yields the same thing as substituting a $y$ for every / in $x$.

But, more deeply, it is not at all obvious from the description I gave of the series of stroke-object sequences that 'multiplication' is, so far, well-defined, and this because I have not in any way given principles of reasoning, a Val, which fix the series as an object. One can indeed institute principles of reasoning which fix the series in such a way that multiplication is well-defined, and so that our proposed theorem has a definite sense. But our description is quite compatible with other ideas. Of special interest are those developed by Rashevskii in his 'On the dogma of the natural numbers':[6]

6 P. K. Rashevskii, 'On the dogma of the natural numbers', *Russian Mathematical Surveys*, vol. 28, no. 4 (1973), pp. 143–8 (p. 144).

The process of real counting of physical objects in sufficiently simple cases is carried through to the end, and leads to a uniquely defined result (the number of people in a hall, for example). The theory of the natural numbers takes this situation to be the fundamental one, and extends it in idealized form 'to infinity'. Roughly speaking, large sets are assumed to be in some sense just as amenable to counting as small ones, and to give just as unique a result. In this sense our assumption on the natural numbers is like looking at a panorama, say of some historical battle. In the foreground, on the real earth are real objects; wrecked guns, blasted trees, etc.; then all this imperceptibly changes into painted canvas, carefully calculated to deceive even the most attentive eye.

Within the framework of a mathematical theory, such an idealization of the process of counting is, of course, quite legitimate. But since there is only the one theory, this point of view automatically becomes imposed upon physics too; however, here the problem takes a quite different turn. For suppose that we wish to know how many gas molecules there are in a given container. Do we have to seek an answer in the form of a completely precisely defined integer? We leave aside the question whether such 'accuracy' is unnecessary for physics, and shall not concern ourselves with the actual difficulty of the problem. Far more important for us is the fact that it is unfeasible in principle; the molecules of the gas interact with the walls of the chamber, undergo various transformations, etc., and hence our problem simply has no definite meaning . . . What would correspond to the spirit of physics would be a mathematical theory of the integers in which numbers, when they became very large, would acquire, in some sense, a 'blurred' form and would not be strictly defined members of the sequence of natural numbers as we consider it.

Indeed, if we consider the series of sequences of stroke-objects, there are at least two views which could be taken about what happens as the sequences get longer. One view, which keeps explicitly in mind the process of construction, holds that $x$ is distinct from $x/$; the other, based on noticing that as the sequences $x$ get longer, it is increasingly difficult to distinguish $x$ from $x/$, or to see that they are different just by looking at them. The latter view corresponds more or less to that suggested by Rashevskii. Thus we have *ideas* for different kinds of objects; but these remain merely ideas until we have instituted principles of reasoning compatible with them. Rashevskii made some proposals for instituting such principles of reasoning making genuine objects of his 'blurred' numbers, but his proposals are little more than vague hints. Nevertheless the possibility at least remains of instituting such principles.

We can say that in general, as far as perceptual intuitions and their imaginative extensions are concerned, there are many different paths open to elementary mathematics; they may be suggestive of many different mathematics, even of hitherto undreamt-of mathematics (such as that proposed by Rashevskii), provided that our so to speak 'logical imagination' is equal to the task (which it may very well not be in the case of Rashevskii's proposal).

Finally, it is worth observing that we can give a rather natural characterization of when a $\mathrm{Val}_O$ is mathematical. Let $A$ be any possible but not necessarily achieved act of consciousness. Then for any proposition $S$, we should be able to determine whether or not $A$ is in the relation $\mathrm{Val}_O$ to $S$, i.e. whether or not $\mathrm{Val}_O(A,S)$. Suppose that it is. In general, as in the case of empirical domains, this alone is not sufficient for us to be justified in asserting $S$. Usually, in order for us to be justified in asserting $S$, we have to achieve or actualize $A$, e.g. we must have the perception $A$ or make the observation $A$. What is characteristic of mathematics is that we only require that $\mathrm{Val}_O(A,S)$ in order to be justified in asserting $S$; we do not have to actualize $A$. This captures the notion that mathematics is somehow *a priori*.

## 5

# PHENOMENOLOGICAL ONTOLOGY AND THE LAW OF THE EXCLUDED MIDDLE

Let us recapitulate and draw some conclusions from our considerations so far. Phenomenology is a philosophical theory of the *cogito*, the 'I think'. For Husserl, every instance of the *cogito* is an act of intentional consciousness, and vice versa. Those acts of consciousness have the character of being directed toward objects; they in some measure posit objects. In each act of intentional consciousness, each instance of the 'I think', something is thought, thought about the posited object. What is in this way thought is called 'the noema' of the act. A crucial aspect of this noema is that it in some respects frames or fixes the intended object of the act. It may happen that when the noema is articulated, when it is brought to expression, we see that part of these expressions are descriptions of the object. But if the intended object is to be a genuine object, if it can have 'true being' for us, then as part of the full articulation of the noema we should find principles for reasoning about the object, principles for thinking further about it, principles of *Evidenz*. It may happen that some or all of the descriptions are wrong; it is on the basis of the principles of reasoning that we can correct them.

From the widest viewpoint, the situation is as follows. For an instance of the *cogito*, we have an intended object. Let us express the latter by '$O$'. $O$ may be an objective domain ('world') or an object or purported object within an objective domain. We express the principles of reasoning by '$\text{Val}_O$'. This expresses a relation between mental performances, $A$, and sentences relevant to $O$, $S$. If $\text{Val}_O(A,S)$ holds, then an occurrence of the mental performance $A$ 'validates' $S$, or

112

makes $S$ 'acceptable'. $A$ may consist in perceptions, observations, reflections, inferences, and so on, or perhaps complex agglomerations of these. I have used the term 'validation'
because it echoes Husserl's use of it, especially in *FTL*. For
Husserl, for $S$ to be validated is for $S$ to be true. But this is
'truth' in a weak sense, but a sense which Husserl regards as
basic: to be true in this sense means just being acceptable
according to given principles of reasoning. The main problem
for us is determining when validation entails *objective truth*,
when the principles of reasoning are of such a nature that, if $S$
is validated by the achievement of some mental performance
$A$ such that $Val_O(A,S)$, we may regard $S$ as having been true
antecedently to the achievement of $A$, or as being true
independently of $A$.

Phenomenology rejects the presumption of our having
available to us an absolute point of view, a point of view presenting us with objective existents, on the one hand, and
language or meanings, on the other, and then determining or
fixing their relationships. (Such a viewpoint is presumed in
correspondence theories of truth.) We have only meanings
and validations; whatever objects there are for us are constituted or made manifest on the basis of the latter. I expressed
this by:

*no entity (for us) antecedently to a way of thinking and to thinking in that
way*

In Chapter 1, I gave a criterion for the justifiability of assertions of existence relative to accumulations and prospec-
tive further accumulations of validations. I raised there the
question of what might compel us to regard objects, whose
existence we are justified in asserting, as real, as objectively
existent, as existing independently of our being justified in
asserting their existence. In what follows I will consider these
matters a little more closely, and the strong suggestion will
emerge that we will never be compelled to regard them in this
way, although there might be no contradiction involved in
regarding some objects as real, as objective existents. Chapters 3

and 4 gave us some idea of how a circumstance in which it was consistent to adopt a realist attitude might arise. Let me briefly consider the explorations there in highly simplified outline.

We began with domains of apparently sense-perceived objects, such as colored objects with sensed colors, cut-out squares with markings of various sorts (e.g. arrows), drawn figures. We assumed *vis-à-vis* Berkeleian considerations that such objects are dependent on our minds for their being because they are given on the basis of sensations. Each such domain $D$ has its $Val_D$ by which we constitute or manifest its objects and have them as objects of thought. We implicitly associated with each $Val_D$ a language or discourse for expressing things about $D$. I sketched (briefly in Chapter 3, more extensively in Chapter 4) how the respective principles of reasoning $Val_D$ and, correlatively, $L_D$ can be modified to produce a new $Val_{D'}$ and correlative $L_{D'}$ constitutive of a domain (e.g. the topological 2-manifolds) whose objects (a) were not sense-perceivable, (b) could be cogently and consistently thought about and (c) were related to the objects of $D$ (by working backwards through the paths of modifications). These principles could be used to acquire insights into, and to develop ideas for further properties of, the objects of $D'$ (in the sense of Chapter 2, the objects in $D$ could be reinterpreted, i.e. looked at from the point of view of their relevance to understanding $D'$). But no sentence of $L_{D'}$ is dependent on sentences of $L_D$ for its validation, although their sense is in some measure 'non-independent' (Husserl's term) of the senses of sentences of $L_D$, for their meaning was created by modifying $Val_D$ in such a way that the reflections on $D$ can be used to acquire insights into $D'$, e.g. as one uses drawings to discover proofs in Euclidean geometry.

The objects of $D'$ are not sensory objects (although by virtue of the nature of the genesis of the constitution of $D'$, i.e. the construction and utilization of $Val_{D'}$, they are related to sensory objects, as indicated above). Furthermore, if $L_{D'}$ contains any idiom of construction, this could be eliminated in favor of an idiom of existence (as, in Hilbert's reconstruction of

Euclid's geometry,[1] theorems about the construction of figures are replaced by theorems about the existence of figures). In this way, $D'$ can be thought about in a perfectly adequate way without (1) ascribing sensory properties to the objects of $D'$, and without (2) regarding the objects of $D'$ as entities we construct. Since (1) and (2) seem to be the only grounds on which there is an issue of the mind-dependence of objects, it seems that we could consistently regard $D'$ as objectively existent, as real, assuming that we find ourselves justified in asserting its existence.[2]

Before examining the role of the law of the excluded middle in determining or making manifest what is real, I should like to examine a bit more closely the extent of our commitment to purported objects as existing objects when we find ourselves justified in asserting their existence. A look at some of Husserl's texts will help us out.

The criterion for the justified assertability of the existence of purported objects which I gave in Chapter 1 was inspired by the following observations from Husserl's *ID*, para. 49:

What is transcendent is given through certain connected experiences. Given directly and with increasing completeness through perceptual continua harmoniously developed, and through certain methodic thought-forms grounded in experience, it reaches ever more fully and immediately theoretic determinations of increasing transparency and unceasing progressiveness. Let us assume that consciousness with its experiential content and progression is really so articulated that the subject of consciousness in the free condition of being able to continue such experience and relevant experiential thinking could carry all such associations and relationships to completion . . . let us further assume that the relevant regulations and requirements of consciousness are actually satisfied ad infinitum, and that as regards the course of consciousness, nothing fails which might in any way be required for the appearance of a unitary world and the rational theoretical knowledge of it. We ask now, presupposing all of

1 David Hilbert, *Foundations of geometry* (La Salle, Ill., 1971).

2 Although this is quite difficult, nothing seems to stand in the way of establishing it with great rigor. What is required is a very meticulous analysis of the respective $Val_D$s and their transformations into the respective $Val_{D'}$'s, perhaps one of the more interesting tasks remaining for phenomenological research.

this, is it still conceivable, is it not on the contrary absurd or non-sensical, *that the corresponding transcendent world should not be?*[3]

I have analyzed this passage in the following way.

Consider a purported objective domain (world) $O$. Suppose that we are able somehow to set out all possible relevant yes-or-no questions $S$? pertaining to this domain. Suppose, further, (1) that we are able to convince ourselves that for every such question, we could think of or form an adequate conception of acts of consciousness, mental performances, $A$, such that $A$ would validate $S$ or validate not-$S$ (i.e. $Val_O(A,S)$ or $Val_O(A, \text{not-}S)$), but that (2) we could also convince ourselves that for each $S$ we could in principle achieve an $A$ which validated either $S$ or not-$S$. Suppose that we could go on to convince ourselves that the accumulating set of validated $S$s were consistent and would remain so under all future extensions. Then, Husserl asks, would it not be absurd to say that $O$ does not exist?

In order to appreciate what makes it compelling to answer that it would be absurd to say that $O$ does not exist, consider a particular act of intentional consciousness in which an entity $O$ is posited. Suppose that one manages to continue thinking about the purported object, accumulating more and more validated sentences about it, satisfying Husserl's demands elaborated above. In this thinking, it indeed *appears* that one is thinking about something. If Husserl's demands are met, then in effect nothing has happened, and nothing can happen, to reveal that the apparent object is only an illusory object. Husserl wrote:

The living intentionality carries me along; it predelineates; it determines me practically in my whole procedure, including the procedure of my natural thinking, whether this yields being or illusion. The living intentionality does all that, even though, as actually functioning, it may be non-thematic, undisclosed.

I said *illusion* as well as *being*. For naturally it is characteristic of the

3 I have made certain changes in Gibson's translation. For a discussion of this passage and the related literature see Karl Ameriks, 'Husserl's realism', *Philosophical Review*, vol. 86, no. 4 (1977), pp. 498–519.

performance-of-consciousness effected by experience itself that, on the one hand, only harmonious experience has the style of performance predelineated as normal for experience and that, on the other hand, its harmony can be broken, that experience can fall into pieces in *conflict*. (*FTL*, para. 94)

The principles of validation $Val_O$ may be defective, permitting the validation of a sentence and its negation. Then $O$ has only illusory being, an illusion we may not ever notice as an illusion because we never actually notice that such 'discordant' validations can be made. In which case we never see 'the cracks in the foundations which tell us that the world is false'. But to the extent that we are convinced that no such conflicts can be brought about (except through error due to our having failed to fully explicate what we intend), we must speak of being or existence rather than illusion. Nothing external to the developing validations and the principles of validation can have a bearing on our determining the existence and nature of purported objects.

There is no conceivable place where the life of consciousness is broken through, or could be broken through, and we might come upon a transcendency that possibly had any sense other than that of an intentional unity making its appearance in the subjectivity itself of consciousness. (*Ibid.*)

Thus, given the satisfaction of Husserl's criterion for the justifiability of assertions of existence, it would indeed be absurd not to regard ourselves as justified in asserting the existence of $O$, and, correlatively, it would also be absurd not to regard the accumulating validated sentences as truths. Since the relevant $Val_O$ determines all considerations which are relevant to the domain $O$ as intended, as meant, there cannot be anything more decisive for the question of the existence of the domain (or objects in it) than Husserl's criterion for the justifiability of assertions of existence:

Whatever I encounter as an existing object is something that (as I must recognize when I systematically explicate my own conscious life, *as a life of validation* [*Geltungsleben*]) has received its *whole* being-sense for me from my effective intentionality. Precisely this I must consult, I must explicate systematically, if I intend to understand what I am allowed, and what I am not allowed, to attribute to an object . . . according to the constituting intentionality from which, as just now said, its whole sense originates. (*Ibid.*)

A life of validation is that aspect of life which consists in validating, e.g. validating sentences. To repeat once more: in order to understand what validations are admitted for any purported object or object sphere, I must reflect on my intentions, on what I mean by the object or objective domain, on the framing noema. What I in the first place mean is explicated by explicating the conditions of validation, the principles of *Evidenz*, of reason, determined by the relevant noematic senses, by which I mean or think this rather than that. Nothing can have a bearing on the meant or intended or thought objects or object spheres except what is provided for in these senses.

As in everyday life, so too in science (*unless, under the misguidance of 'realistic' epistemology, it misinterprets its own doing*) experience is the consciousness of being with the matters themselves, of seizing upon and having them quite directly. But experience is not an opening through which a world, existing prior to all experience, shines into a room of consciousness. (*Ibid.*, my italics)

Rather, experience is 'validating experience'; objects and a world can only be meant as entities which can be thought of and experienced in such and such a way (according to the principles of validation); they are what is thought and experienced in such and such a way, and cannot be conceived antecedently to or independently of such thinking and such experiencing (as determined by the principles of validation).

The 'realist epistemology' Husserl inveighs against envisages 'the world', on the one hand, and experience or consciousness, on the other hand, and then confronts the problem of how we could ever acquire knowledge of 'the world'. The error here is the analogue of the error of those who try to institute a correspondence theory of truth, who presume a point of view which they do not have, an absolute point of view giving 'the world' independently of that through which 'the world' has a meaning for us, namely, the thoughts through which we think 'it' and the principles of validation regulative of such thinking.

any straightforwardly constituted objectivity (for example: an object belonging to Nature) points back, according to its essential sort (for example: physical thing *in specie* [the conception 'physical thing']), to a correlative essential form of manifold (actual and possible) intentionality . . . which is constitutive for that objectivity. The multiplicity of possible perceptions, memories, and, indeed, intentional processes of whatever sort, that relate, or can relate, 'harmoniously' to one and the same physical thing has (in all of its tremendous complication) a quite definite essential character, which is identical in the case of *any* physical thing whatever and is particularized only according to the different individual things constituted in different cases. (*FTL*, para. 98)

The 'essential form of manifold' is exactly what I have been calling the principles of validation, which I have expressed canonically by 'Val'. Husserl is here pointing out that there is a Val for each individual, but that this itself is simply a specialization of the $Val_{world-of-physical-objects}$. What we mean by 'a physical object' is fixed and determined by just such principles of validation. With every essential sort of objectivity (e.g. 'physical thing') there is an essential manifold of intentionality (viz. all of the actual and possible validating acts $A$ such that for some relevant $S$, $A$ validates $S$).

Although in this passage Husserl is only using the example of 'the physical world', in the very next sentences he indicates that the same considerations apply to all purported worlds or objective domains, even domains of 'ideal' or mathematical objects:

In the same fashion, the modes of consciousness that can make one aware of some ideal objectivity or other, and can become united as a synthetic consciousness of it, have a definite character, essential to *this* sort of objectivity. (*Ibid.*)

We are so to speak free to entertain as many objective domains or worlds as our 'logical imagination' is powerful, or as our ability to achieve or construct principles of validation leading to the satisfaction of the criterion for the justifiability of assertions of existence will allow.

What now of the justification of an attitude of realism toward an objective domain? Suppose that we are in the situation envisaged earlier in the chapter of finding that nothing contradicts our construing an objective domain $D'$ as real. We construe the logical syntax of $L_{D'}$ to be that of classical objectual quantificational logic, for which the law of the excluded middle is valid. If we are justified in asserting the existence of $D'$, then there is nothing to conflict with our asserting that here we are in the presence of an objective reality.

Not only is there nothing to conflict with this, but there is no standpoint from which to discredit such an assertion, discrediting it, say, as a mere fiction. There is no absolute point of view available to us. Any objective domain is manifest to us only through our validations.

The circumstance might arise that there are many worlds or objective domains which we may regard as existing and real. If this circumstance arises, then we could not regard any one as *the* real world. Classical logical theory (realist logic), a theory in which the law of the excluded middle is the fundamental principle, clearly manifests itself as a kind of *formal ontology*, a matter discussed at length in Husserl's *FTL*. It expresses so to speak the realist conception of truth and thus of being. It is a formal ontology, determining the 'formal *a priori*' of 'the objectively real'. Since any ontological region or world is constituted, made manifest, on the basis of some relation of validation Val, if that relation is constrained to be of such a nature that the thoughts which can be validated on its basis may be consistently regarded as satisfying the law of the excluded middle, then, if we are justified in asserting that the purported domain exists, we may regard it as objectively real, but nothing in this circumstance forces us to regard the law of the excluded middle as a necessary law for all objective domains. Thus we may also have objective domains which are not objectively real.

Let us grant that it could happen that there are many domains of objects which we could regard as objectively real, with the result that we cannot speak of 'objective reality' as something unique, as one unified whole. What then?

As long as one moved within a metaphysical vision of there being such an objective reality, '*the* real world', there would be a considerable interest in sustaining and justifying a realism in mathematics, such a mathematics forming in some way the mathematics of 'the real world'. If we have no authority to speak of *the* real world, then there are no grounds for an interest in a single mathematical reality as a part of a full and unified objective reality. Indeed, as has become increasingly clear with the advent of intuitionistic mathematics, wherein the law of the excluded middle is not valid, the confinement of mathematics to theories with a classical logical syntax represents a great restriction on the mathematical imagination. With the emergence of, say, topos theory, which puts the classical concept of set in a very general context, the law of the excluded middle is found to be a consequence of certain strong assertions about the existence of mathematical objects (e.g. the axiom of choice). This makes this law subservient to the mathematical imagination, e.g. subservient to a desire on the part of a mathematician to consider mathematical domains where certain strong symmetries or correspondences between objects exist.

Does the problem of realism or anti-realism cease to be of any significance? While its interest for mathematics is evaporating, it is nevertheless still of great interest with respect to what we vaguely refer to as the world about us. It is at the very least of great practical interest for us to determine which aspects, if any, are of our making, are our responsibility. But how do we go about determining those aspects?

In his *Crisis of the European sciences and transcendental phenomenology*, Husserl sketched an answer to this question. We may explain it in the following way:

'The world about us' Husserl characterized as our 'lived-world', the world in which we live and act. This world is itself noematically constituted by us; there is some (very complex) $Val_{lived-world}$ where the relevant language, $L_{lived-world}$ is our ordinary language. The reader will recall the sketches of ways of modifying a $Val_D$ in Chapter 4, where $D$ was indeed an aspect of our lived-world, into a $Val_{D'}$, where $D'$ was a mathematical world (e.g. the world of 2-manifolds). $D'$ could not be considered to be an aspect of the world we find ourselves in (e.g. at the very least, we cannot construct Klein bottles). Husserl was convinced that, given a very meticulous and thorough analysis of $Val_{lived\text{-}world}$, we could see clearly how to produce modifications $Val_N$ in which $N$ would have the clear sense of being an aspect of the world we find ourselves in. All possible $Val_N$s for which we are justified in asserting the existence of $N$ would then determine all possible 'natural sciences', but these would not be 'sciences in crisis', for their relation to the sphere of our life, the world about us, would be exactly determined. If, furthermore, a $Val_N$ for which we were justified in asserting the existence of $N$ was fully consistent with the law of the excluded middle (in the sense discussed in the first part of this chapter), then we could rightfully regard $N$ as objectively real, as an aspect of our lived-world not of our making, as something for which we are not responsible. But carrying out this program is no easy matter, however much it is prima facie in our interest to do so. Perhaps we could learn how to carry it out, as Husserl himself believed, by continuing the work in some small way begun in the last chapter, of working out in full detail the modifications which take us from $Val_{lived\text{-}world}$ to $Val_{Euclidean\ geometry}$.

# BIBLIOGRAPHY

Ameriks, Karl. 'Husserl's realism', *Philosophical Review*, vol. 86, no. 4 (1977), pp. 498–519.

Berg, Jan. *Bolzano's logic*, Stockholm, n.d. but *circa* 1968.

Bolzano, Bernard. *Paradoxes of the infinite*, trans. Fr Prihousky, New Haven, Conn., 1950.

    *Theory of science*, ed. Jan Berg, trans. Burnham Terrell, Boston, Mass., 1973.

Brouwer, L. E. J. *Collected works I*, ed. A. Heyting, Amsterdam, 1975.

    'On the foundations of mathematics' (dissertation), in *Collected works I*, pp. 11–101.

    'Consciousness, philosophy and mathematics', in *Collected works I*, pp. 480–94.

Davidson, Donald. 'Truth and meaning', *Synthese*, vol. 7 (1967), pp. 304–23.

Dummett, Michael. *Truth and other enigmas*, London, 1978.

    'Realism', in his *Truth and other enigmas*, pp. 145–65.

    'Platonism', in his *Truth and other enigmas*, pp. 202–14.

    *Frege*, 2nd edn, London, 1981.

Føllesdal, Dagfinn. 'Husserl's notion of noema', *Journal of Philosophy*, vol. 66 (1969), pp. 680–7.

    'Phenomenology for analytic philosophers', in *Philosophy in Scandinavia*, ed. R. Olsen and A. Paul, Baltimore, Md., 1972, pp. 417–29.

Frege, Gottlob. 'Begriffsschrift', trans. S. Bauer-Mengelberg, in *From Frege to Gödel*, ed. van Heijenoort, Cambridge, Mass., 1981, pp. 1–82.

    'Thoughts', in his *Logical investigations*, trans. P. T. Geach and R. H. Stoothoff, Oxford, 1977, pp. 1–30.

    'Sources of knowledge of mathematics and the mathematical natural sciences', in his *Posthumous writings*, trans. P. Long and R. White, Oxford, 1979, pp. 267–74.

    *Foundations of arithmetic*, trans. J. L. Austin, New York, 1950.

Gödel, Kurt. 'What is Cantor's continuum problem?', in *Philosophy of mathematics*, ed. P. Benacerraf and H. Putnam, Englewood Cliffs, N.J., 1964, pp. 258–74.

Hersh, Reuben. 'Some proposals for reviving the philosophy of mathematics', *Advances in Mathematics*, vol. 31, no. 1 (1979), pp. 31–50.

Hilbert, David. 'On the infinite', in *From Frege to Gödel*, pp. 367–93.
*Foundations of geometry*, La Salle, Ill., 1971.
and S. Cohn-Vossen. *Geometry and the imagination*, New York, 1952.

Husserl, Edmund. *Philosophie der Arithmetik, Husserliana*, The Hague, 1970.
*Logical investigations*, trans. J. Findlay, New York, 1970.
*Ideas*, trans. W. R. B. Gibson, New York, 1969.
*Formal and transcendental logic*, trans. D. Cairns, The Hague, 1969.
*Cartesian Meditations*, trans. D. Cairns, The Hague, 1960: *Cartesianische Meditationen, Husserliana I*, The Hague, 1963.
*Crisis of the European sciences and transcendental phenomenology*, trans. David Carr, Evanston, Ill., 1970: *Die Krisis der europäischen Wissenschaften und die transcendentale Phänomenologie, Husserliana*, The Hague, 1954.
*Introduction to the logical investigations – a draft preface (1913)*, trans. P. J. Bossert and C. H. Peters, The Hague, 1975.

Kleene, S. C. *Introduction to metamathematics*, New York, 1962.

Lotze, Hermann. *Logic*, trans. B. Bosanquet, Oxford, 1898.

McIntyre, R. and Smith, D. 'Husserl's identification of meaning and noema', *The Monist*, vol. 59 (1975) pp. 115–33.
'Intentionality via intensions', *Journal of Philosophy*, vol. 68 (1971), pp. 541–61.

Massey, W. S. *Algebraic topology: an introduction*, Berlin, 1967.

Rashevskii, P. K. 'On the dogma of the natural numbers', *Russian Mathematical Surveys*, vol. 28, no. 4 (1973), pp. 143–8.

Tarski, Alfred. 'What is elementary geometry?' in *The philosophy of mathematics*, ed. J. Hintikka, Oxford, 1969, pp. 164–75.

Tragesser, R. *Phenomenology and logic*, Ithaca, N.Y., 1977.

Willard, Dallas. 'Husserl on a logic that failed', *Philosophical Review*, vol. 89, no. 1 (1980), pp. 46–64.

# INDEX

Ameriks, K., 116
anti-realism, xiii-xiv, 24, 27, 38, 42, 70; and Brouwer, xiv; *see also* existence, realism, truth

being, conception of (*Seinsinn*), 24, 35, 38, 42, 44, 117
Berkeley, G., 15-16, 33-4, 97
Bolzano, B., 38; and Cantor, 1; and Frege, xiii, 1-3; and Husserl, 6, 11; and Kant, xiii, 1-2
bracketing (of existence), 17, 22
Brentano, F., 9
Brouwer, L. E. J., xiv, 37-8, 50

Cantor, G., xiv, 1, 40, 45, 50
*cogito*, the (the 'I think'), xiii, xvi, 5, 9, 80, 112

Davidson, D., 28-9
Derrida, J., 104
Dieudonné, J., 43-4, 50
Dummett, M., 45, 70; and Brouwer, xiv; and realism/anti-realism, xiii-xv, 70; on Frege, 31

empiricism, 71, 73
epistemology, 42, 118
Euclid (Euclidean geometry), 43, 45ff, 75, 101, 106-9, 115
*Evidenz* (the ground of rationality in relation to intentionality), 1, 27, 52, 75, 77, 102-3, 107, 112
excluded middle, law of the, xiii, xvi, 2, 11, 28ff, 115ff
existence, as true being, 13-14
existence, justified assertability of, criterion for, 23, 115

Formalism, 43ff

formal meaning: *see* meaning
foundedness, 16, 35, 55, 107; *see also* interpreted object, intuition
Frazer spirals, 61ff
Frege, G., xv, 1-4, 39; and realist concepts, 34; and the inadequacy of intuition to meaning, 26; and the third realm, 2, 10, 26; his rejection of the correspondence theory of truth, 2-3, 80; *see also* Bolzano, Husserl, Kant
fulfillability, 12-13, 31-2; *see also* Val, validation

Gödel, K., 39-40

Hersh, R., 42f
Hilbert, D., 1, 53-4, 114
Hjelmslev, J., 98, 101-2, 108-9
Husserl, E., xvi-xvii, 42, 57, 66, 75, 80-3, 90, 97, 102, 112ff; and Bolzano, 6, 11; and Brentano, 9; and Frege, 6, 60; and logic, 2, 115ff

illusion, 18, 21-2, 43, 61ff, 97, 116ff
infinity (mathematical), 1, 37-9; and meaning, xiii-xiv; *see also* mathematics
intensionality (conceptual meaning), 10; *see also* sense
intentionality (mental directedness toward something), 11, 14, 21-2, 32-3, 60, 80, 112; as a trait of the *cogito*, xvi; connection with metaphysics, 35; *see also cogito*
interpreted objects, 16, 55ff, 67, 72, 78; *see also* foundedness, intuition
intuition, 2, 15-16, 37, 51ff; and foundedness, 35; *see also* foundedness, interpreted objects

125